C-128 CP/M USER'S GUIDE

A revealing look into CP/M on the C-128

By Jörg Schieb
and Elmar A. Weiler

A Data Becker Book

Published by

Abacus Software

First Printing, March 1986
Printed in U.S.A.

ISBN 0-916439-45-3

Foreword

The Commodore 128 is an exciting, unique computer. It provides three completely independent modes of operation: the 64 mode, the 128 mode, and the CP/M mode. Each of these modes has its interesting applications and deserves attention. The 128's forerunner, the Commodore C-64, has an enormous amount of software available for it. All of it can run on the 128 with complete compatibility to the 64 mode. New software written for the enhanced features found in 128 mode are appearing every day. Finally, the 128's CP/M mode, though often overlooked by owners and software developers alike, has many very important and exciting possiblities.

Like the weather, everyone seems to talk about the 128's CP/M mode, but no one does anything about it. Does that mean its CP/M isn't any good? On the contrary. While the CP/M for the Commodore 64, CP/M 2.2, had its difficulties, the 128 KBytes RAM with the C-128 makes it possible to run CP/M 3.0 (also known as CP/M Plus). CP/M 3.0 performs much better than the old CP/M 2.2.

The C-128 also has other inviting features. It has a fantastic keyboard that's especially suitable here for long hours of programming. Some subtle but very convenient ideas went into it. For example, the keys F and J are provided with a small dot in the middle, so that you can more easily place your fingers in the correct position on the keyboard without looking. The Commodore developers have had a bit more experience designing computers than a lot of newcomers. Several competitors have a mouse to offer, but have really poor quality keyboards—and working with a bad keyboard is about as inviting as eating in a dirty restaurant.

The C-128's companion, the 1571 disk drive, offers a lot of performance and value for the money. Theoretically you can work with CP/M 3.0 on your old 1541, but this would greatly reduce the efficiency of the sytem. An upgrade to the 1571 will save you many hours of waiting, in the long run.

Those who predict the death of CP/M caused by its new rival, GEM, will have to be patient for a few more years. There's a lot of CP/M software out there, all readily available to any computer equipped with CP/M. The 68000-chip computers have it pretty tough, because completely new software must be developed for them.

The purpose of this book is to show you how to work with CP/M as comfortably and quickly as possible. All of the standard CP/M commands, as well those CP/M commands peculiar to the Commodore 128, are thoroughly explained.

We hope you have a lot of fun with CP/M on your Commodore 128, and much success applying it.

Sincerely,

E. A. Weiler
J. Schieb

Düsseldorf, W. Germany
November 1985

Chapter One

The Computer

The Computer

We don't know how familiar you are with computers. Unfortunately we can't ask each reader individually. So we'll start at the beginning with fundamental computer concepts so we can all start this book on equal footing.

First of all, what is a computer? We'll try to answer this question scientifically.

The word itself, "computer" tells us what it does. A computer is a calculator—it computes. Such a computing machine can do great many things, such as process a lot of numbers in accounting and calculate the totals of ledger columns.

1.1 The keyboard

But we have a problem. In front of us is a box that supposedly can calculate. How do we tell it *what* it should calculate? It would be nice if we could just instruct it verbally, but that's still a few years down the road. Therefore we have the next-best alternative, the good old typewriter keyboard, and use it to enter information into our computing machine.

Since the computer has many more functions than a typewriter, its keyboard is somewhat different. A computer keyboard has between 60 and 100 or so keys, depending on its price and features. Since the Commodore 128 is a many-featured computer, it is equipped with a numeric keypad for inputting a large amount of numbers. The small mark in the middle of the 5-key serves as orientation for your fingers on the numeric keypad when you are not looking at it. By the way, you'll also find this small mark on the F and J keys to guide your fingers.

A few often-used keys are especially important. We'll describe them now, along with their uses.

RETURN

You'll recognize this key from the typewriter. With the C-128 and other computers it's often used in different ways. The designations for this key are:

<RETURN>

<ENTER>

CR (abbreviation for carriage return)

BACK SPACING

<BS> (back space)

<- (cursor left)

DELETION OR CORRECTION KEYS

<DELETE>

DEL (abbreviation for DELETE)

RUB OUT

SHIFT / UPPER CASE

<SHIFT> (turns on capitalization)

LOCK

<SHIFT LOCK> (continuous <SHIFT>)

The actual function of this key depends on the computer. This key usually doesn't change the way the whole keyboard functions. It means that only capital letters are printed when a *letter* key is pressed. It can make your typing work a lot easier.

The Commodore 128, on the other hand, uses <SHIFT LOCK> to change the function of *all* keys on the keyboard. It's the same as holding down the <SHIFT> key.

CAPS LOCK

Normally the C-128's <CAPS LOCK> key only affects the letter keys, but in CP/M it is inoperative.

CONTROL

The <CONTROL> key, is on the left side of your C-128 keyboard. It is used for many control commands in conjuction with letter or digit keys.

1.2 The Screen

Actually the title of this section should be plural: *The Screens.* That's because the C-128 use two screens at the same time. After we've put data in the computer, we obviously need a way to display that information. It doesn't help us much if the computer makes a lot of wonderful calculations if it has no way of telling us what it's done. Data output on a screen is nice, because it's fast and doesn't make any noise. Data and error messages from the computer are quickly shown, and if you want a hardcopy of your mistakes, we can always send them to a printer.

The screen itself is basically similar to a television set. It is often called a monitor, and displays letters, digits, and other characters. The monitor is different from a TV set in that it usually has a better resolution, making it easier on the eyes of the user.

1.3 The Printer

The computer can send its data to a printer for permanent record of its data. The first large computers, which performed quite slowly by today's standards, used telex machines to output for permanent paper copies. These telex machines were very loud, and wasted a lot of paper.

The disadvantages of printers, noise and paper waste, are still with us today in varying degrees. But many people need their computer information in printed form, so they need to use a printer. Since there are so many different printers on the market today, we'll give you a short overview.

Printer prices and performance vary widely. They cost from $50 to $8000 and up. They can print between 15 and 800 characters per second, depending on their cost.

1.3.1 The Dot-matrix Printer

Dot-matrix printers work especially well with microcomputers like the C-128. They are the most popular, best-selling printers, due to the fact that they are among the lowest priced printers. In addition, dot-matrix printers do their work faster than many other types of printers. Dot-matrix printers print dots very closely together to form letters and characters. Wire needles strike a ribbon against the paper to produce a tiny dot. A minimum of seven dots are required to produce a letter, digit or other character. In the early days of personal computing (before 1980 or so), the quality of these printers was very poor. It was quite hard to read its text if the printout is of any great length.

But those days are past. There are still very cheap models of dot-matrix printers on the market today that print 80 to 100 characters per second. They aren't good enough for correspondence, but are sufficient for some applications. A big advantage of dot-matrix printers is that you have a choice of fonts, and can even program your own fonts—for example, to include foreign language characters. This makes written correspondence with Germany, Greece or Japan much easier.

High performance dot-matrix printers print up to 800 characters per second with 132 dots across the width of the character. They vary in cost from about $500 to $3000. This new breed of dot-matrix printers have become available only recently. They usually have 24 print needles, and can approach the quality of typewriter print (at reduced speed). Customarily they print about 50 characters per second for correspondence, and 140 to 150 characters per second in quick-print mode.

1.3.2 The daisy-wheel printer

A second type of printer is the daisy-wheel printer. This group includes the ball-head printers. These printers are typically based on obsolete typewriter designs, and require a lot of costly maintenance. Their large number of moving parts make them quite expensive to manufacture.

Daisy-wheel printers have a disk that replaces the type-basket or ball head of a conventional typewriter. This disk contains the various letters and characters required for printing on the rim of the disk itself. The disk rotates on its axis, and a small hammer hits the required character against the ribbon, creating an impression on the paper. Daisy-wheel print is indistinguishable from that of a typewriter's. A daisy-wheel printer might be considered if your computer output needs to be letter-quality.

The speed of the cheapest daisy-wheel printer models is about 20 characters per second. Top-of-the-line models can print at about 80 characters per second.

1.3.3 The ink-jet printer

A fairly new type of printer is the ink-jet printer. These are a lot cheaper than daisy-wheel printers. Like a dot-matrix printer, it prints letters and digits using little dots. However, there are no mechanical parts between the print head and the paper. Instead, little drops of ink are "sprayed" at the paper. Its print quality is comparable to that of a cheaper dot-matrix printer. The big advantage of ink-jet printers is that they are very quiet. Printing about 150 characters per second, their noise level is very low. Their major disadvantage is that they can't make multiple copies through carbon paper, such as for printing invoices in triplicate.

1.3.4 The thermal printer

Thermal printers use heat to print the characters on the paper. They require a special type of paper. The paper turns dark after exposure to heat. These printers are quite cheap, and are good enough for everyday functions. The simplest models of thermal printers cost under $100.

Also in this category, but at the other end of the quality and price spectrums, is the laser printer. Laser printers produce the highest-quality print of all computer printers. They use a laser beam to scan across a drum and form characters, which are then printed using a Xerographic process. It's hard to tell a laser printer's copy from typeset print.

You really don't want to know how much laser printers cost. Believe me.

1.4 Data memory

Let's see what makes up our computer so far. We have a keyboard, a screen, and a printer. Now what we need is a place to store the data we which we enter. First we need storage while the data is inside the computer, and then we need long-term storage. We can store the data inside the computer in its memory. For long-term storage we can use a floppy diskette or hard disk. Let's take a look at how a computer stores its data.

1.5 One or zero: Foundations of binary arithmetic

The computer is an electronic device. Because of this, any information inside the computer must be represented in electrical form. But how do we represent it with electricity? How do we tell the computer what we mean? It's essential to have a method of representation that the computer understands. One representation which the computer recognizes is power flow—either the power is on or the power is off. It works on the same principle as a light bulb. When the power is turned on, the filament in the light burns. If you cut off its power source, the light goes out. This simple process is fundamental to the operation of the computer. The computer is wired in such a way that the condition "power on" has the same meaning as the value "1".

Conversely, if no power is flowing, the computer reads this as the value "0". Being able to differentiate between these two states leads to some astonishing effects.

1.6 Counting in binary

The binary number system uses only ones and zeros for counting. It's not especially good for ordinary use—counting aloud in binary from one to a hundred would probably take you several hours. Fortunately, the computer's circuitry can process the two digits of binary number system with incredible speed.

There are several counting systems: binary, decimal, hexadecimal, and others. We all know the decimal system very well. We are accustomed to thinking in the decimal, or base 10, system. In fact, most of us can hardly imagine counting any other way.

So what can we learn from this new system? Think of a decimal number: zero, for instance. If we want a larger number, we can choose one, two, and so on. If we want a number larger than 9, we go to a two-digit number: 10.

We can do something similar when we have only two numbers to work with as in the binary system. The first number, as before, is zero. The next is one. We don't have any more numbers than these to work with, so we immediately go to a two-digit number. We denote the value two as 10. Three is 11. For the number four we have to add a new digit place, and get 100.

Here is a table of binary numbers:

zero	=	0
one	=	1
two	=	10
three	=	11
four	=	100
five	=	101
six	=	110
seven	=	111
eight	=	1000

We must pay attention to the number of places in this counting system. We can represent two numbers with one place, four numbers with two places, eight with three places, sixteen with four places, and so on. The number of numbers that can be represented *doubles* for every place added on. In our decimal system we know how place values work. Each added place in the decimal system allows us to represent *ten times* as many numbers. With one place we can represent 10 numbers, with two places a hundred, with three place a thousand, and so on.

The binary number system proved to be so useful for use with computers that people soon developed technical terms for describing elements of this system. A single place is called a digit. Since there are only two possibilities for each place, it is a binary place. Put together, we get the phrase *binary digit*. We refer to this as a *bit*.

In order to make it easier for the computer to handle these individual bits, they are grouped into a unit of eight bits—a *byte*. If we extend our previous table of binary numbers, we would find that 8 bits, or one byte, can represent 256 values.

1.7 Memory values

The computer must be able to store these numbers. A number is represented by the computer as an electrical condition, a sequence of switches that are on or off. Since one byte isn't a lot of memory, we often refer to a computer's storage capacity in *kilobytes*, or thousands of bytes. To be precise, one kilobyte represents 1024 bytes. A 64,000 byte memory is designated as 64K.

Through electronic switching it is possible to read the value of a byte, to process that value, and to assign it a new value. That is the power of computer. Its advantage is that it can carry out these operations very quickly, making it a very useful data manipulator.

All computer memory has a limited area in which to store data. The typical size for the work memory of a personal computer with an 8-bit processor is 64 kilobytes (or 64K for short). The new 16-bit computers have work memory between 128 K and about eight megabytes. Though the Commodore 128 is an 8-bit machine, it has 128 K of memory—the amount of space needed for CP/M 3.0. You can upgrade it to 512K if you desire.

You might wonder how we can store text in a computer, since it can only accept and output numbers. For this purpose, the computer uses a dictionary, similar to one we would use to translate a foreign language. Within the computer is a table that associates every letter and character with a numeric value. When you type in the letter `T`, for instance, it looks at the table and finds the right value for `T`, and converts it into this binary number. Then it proceeds to read the next character. To output a character to the screen or printer, it reverses the procedure.

To be compatible regardless of the brand or model our computer, manufacturers have agreed upon a standard for the translation table format. Most computers use ASCII (American Standard Code for Information Interchange). The ASCII code contains 128 characters, each of which has its own numeric value. **Appendix A** has a table listing these ASCII values.

A computer's memory, regardless of size, cannot perform work unless there is a set of commands to organize the computer's work. For instance, a command might take a data value in memory location A add it to the value in memory location B and put the sum in memory location C.

The computer's CPU (central processing unit) contains many such commands.

To carry out a particular task, the computer must have an exact list of commands telling it what to do, every step of the way. This list of commands is known as a *program*. A program's commands work in sequence to guide the computer toward its end goal. The program must be resident in the computer's memory to run, and therefore needs memory space.

Depending on the task, such a program will be between 10K and 120K long. Sometimes so much memory space is taken up by the program that there is no room to store your data.

1.8 Mass Storage

It's rarely necessary to have an entire program in the computer's working memory. Usually it's sufficient if the important parts are in work memory and the rest are in storage, ready to be called up when needed. One of the ways a computer does this is with the *overlay* technique. Using this method frees up internal memory, as well as providing additional space for that memory. The mass storage device can be a floppy disk drive or a hard disk drive. Each has its own advantages and disadvantages, but all provide large amounts of space for data, and can exchange that data with the computer in a reasonable amount of time.

1.8.1 The Floppy Diskette

The *floppy diskette*, also referred to as a *floppy* or a *disk*, is made out of a material similar to magnetic tapes. It is a thin disk with a finely polished, high-density magnetic surface. Floppys are enclosed in jackets to protect the disk from small contaminants like dust, dirt and fingerprints. An electronic *read-write head* on the disk drive moves along the disk's surface and magnetizes or demagnetizes different areas.

With a disk we again find two states: magnetized, or not magnetized. There's a good reason for this. The data represented in the computer as electrical states can be directly transferred to the floppy. Data is written to the floppy in a binary technique, as magnetized and non-magnetized spots on the floppy, and is later read back by the computer in a like manner. If a bit is ON, the write head makes a small spot on the disk surface magnetic. If the next bit is OFF, nothing is written on the floppy disk. This corresponds directly with data representation within the computer itself.

The floppy diskette spins rapidly on its axis, making 200 to 300 revolutions per minute. To organize the data on the magnetic surface, the disk is divided into a number of *tracks*, which lie next to each other like lanes on an athletic track.

If we want to put data on the disk, the write head moves over a particular track and writes the data to it.

To reduce the time needed to read and write to different tracks, the disk is divided once again, into *sectors*. These sectors are between 128 and 1024 bytes long, depending on the manufacturer. The Commodore 128 uses a different floppy format in the CP/M mode, to make it compatible with several different CP/M versions. We'll discuss these different formats later.

Unfortunately, disk drives from one computer manufacturer aren't necessarily compatible with another manufacturer's disk drives. Every computer maker uses their own format, much to the chagrin of users. Apple is especially adept at frustrating programmers with its incompatible drives.

For these reasons, floppy disks can't be used straight out of the box. They must first be *formatted* before they can be used. Each computer has its own special program to write to those particular disk tracks and sectors that the computer will use.

You've got to be careful to make sure you don't reformat disks containing important data. Formatting destroys all the data already on a diskette. It's a good idea to put a *write protect tab* on the notch of valuable data disks. These tabs are the small stickers packed in every box of disks. They can save you from the extreme frustration of seeing hours of work wiped out by inadvertent reformatting.

By the way, it is smart always to have a backup copy for all important data stored away, someplace where children, dogs, cats, fire, thieves, snowstorms, and the like can't harm them. Even if you don't keep your diamond jewelry in a safe, at least lock up your backup copies. They are really that important to your programming. If you need help making CP/M backups and other copies, skip ahead to the next chapter for a moment.

At the present time there are a lot of different disk formats on the market. For instance, you can still find the old 8" diskettes, at one time hailed as the state-of-the-art in data processing. The 5 1/4" disks are especially popular, widely used by personal computer users. This format is handy and depending on the computer, you can fit up to two Megabytes on them.

The 3 and 3 1/2" micro-diskettes from Japan promise even more convenience than the 5 1/4" diskettes. These disks have a metal flap that closes access to the actual disk surface when not in use. This prevents almost all contaminants from reaching the magnetic surface. Also, they have a stiff plastic jacket that prevents damage due to accidental bending, folding and other forms of user abuse.

1.8.2 The hard disk

Another type of mass storage device is the *hard disk drive.* Used predominantly with business computers, a hard disk has the same measurements as a 5 1/4" floppy disk (although there are also 3 1/2" hard disk drives). They cannot be inserted and ejected as with normal floppy disks. This is because hard disks are permanently enclosed in a tightly sealed housing, allowing more precision and hence increased rotation speeds. The spinning magnetic disk makes about 3000 rotations per minute as the read/write head glides over the disk surface. A dust or smoke particle on the disk surface would affect the hard disk like a small rock on your stereo turntable.

The standard memory capacity of the hard disk drive so far has been the 10 MByte (megabyte or millions of bytes) drive. But the 20 MB hard disk drive is starting to gain popularity as its price drops.

In addition to its especially large storage capacity, the hard disk drive offers another decided advantage—its can store and retrieve data about 20 times faster than the floppy diskette drive. And the only real disadvantage of hard disk drives is their steep price tags. They cost from $800 to over $5000.

1.9 Summary

Hopefully you've gained an understanding of the fundamental components of a computer system and their operation. Here's a quick review:

- A computer is an electronic calculating machine that uses a keyboard and a monitor screen as input and output devices.
- A printer is another output device used to make permanent copies of a computer's data. The categories of printers include dot-matrix, daisy wheel, ink-jet, and thermal printers, each with their own advantages and disadvantages.
- The computer works with binary numbers. The binary system includes only the numbers one and zero. A computer groups binary digits, or bits, into binary values.
- Floppy disks and hard disks are external storage devices.

In the next chapter we'll examine the operating system and its functions.

Chapter Two

The Operating System

The operating system

In the previous chapter we took a quick look at the computer's hardware—the individual components of a computer. In and of itself, computer hardware has very little value. That's because a computer can't initiate any useful activity. A computer becomes valuable when it is able to run important, useful programs. That is why we need *software*. When talking about software, we must make some differentiations.

We'll discuss two software types: the *operating system* and the *programs*. You should keep it in the back of your mind that the operating system is a program, too. The differentiation is mine. It arises from the function of the two types of software.

We regularly hear inexperienced people who are interested in computers ask: "*Can it also do word processing?*" These people don't understand the difference between a program and an operating system. Therefore we will explain it, in case you are asked the question sometime.

2.1 What is a program?

Essentially, a *program* is a list of tasks which the computer performs sequentially, one after the other. These tasks are specified as instructions that the computer can understand. Since the computer is a machine, this language is called *machine language*. Programs written in machine language are incomprehensible to most "normal" people, but the computer likes them. Since machine language is written in a way that the computer can understand, it performs these instructions very quickly.

To make programming easier for us "normal" people, other programming languages are available. Among these are BASIC, COBOL, FORTRAN, Pascal, and Modula-2. These languages have commands or statements which are more understandable than machine language instructions. These high-level commands are translated or converted into machine language instructions before the computer carries them out.

Any program is nothing more than a sequence of machine language instructions or high-level commands. When you write a program in BASIC for the 128, you are not writing *any* of the instructions that the computer actually carries out. A large number of small tasks are performed by the computer without your knowledge. For example, the computer must determine which key on the keyboard was pressed, which character is to appear on the screen, or what data is to be read from the disk drive.

The computer spends a great deal of time performing these types of activities. To write the instructions to perform these things for each and every program is cumbersome.

2.2 Operating systems

There is a better way to program the computer and avoid repetitive work. We can divide the program into a *main program* and "*often-used routines*." The main program performs tasks such as print a customer invoice or dial a number using a modem. The "often-used routines" perform tasks such as scanning the keyboard for a pressed key or converting a value in memory to an ASCII character.

Collectively these "often-used routines" can perform all of the low-level, frequently used tasks that most programs require. This is then called an *operating system.*

The operating system provides a standardized method for programs to use the commonly used functions. The major task of the operating system is to handle the data transmission between the computer and the peripherals.

In CP/M mode, the 128 uses a very well-known operating system. CP/M is the acronym for Control Program for Microprocessors. CP/M works on 8080, 8085, and Z80 microprocessors.

2.3 CP/M's task

CP/M handles the basic tasks of accepting input of characters, outputting characters, managing the storage areas on the disk drive, and reading from or writing to disks. These routines can be used in a standardized way in all applications programs.

Since this is true, CP/M must do its job in two different modes. It is divided into two large sections. The first section, BDOS (Basic Disc Operating System) takes care of all the tasks which are machine independent. A second part of the CP/M operating system is BIOS (Basic Input/Output System). BIOS handles the program sections which are machine dependent.

Every computer has its own methods of carrying out specific tasks. Consequently, we can't simply take the operating system from one computer and run it on another. Before an operating system is able to run on different computer hardware, a new BIOS must be produced for the computer, since BIOS is dependent on the computer's hardware. You shouldn't have any problem with your C-128, since it's fitted with a functioning operating system.

2.4 Different CP/M versions

Most programs that have been on the computer market for any length of time have improvements made on them. Usually new versions are released. There are no perfect programs, so some of a program's errors may creep in when users try it out and test all its capabilities.

When the software publisher discovers program errors, and the errors are corrected, a new version of the program is usually made available. One version, CP/M 2.2, is practically error-free. It is the standard operating system for many 8-bit computers. The newer version CP/M 3.0 isn't just an upgrade to eliminate errors, but a new version with new features. The new version is aimed at maintaining the life of CP/M with new computers and new computer programming methods.

2.5 The CP/M prompt

Let's leave the theory and talk about the C-128 and the CP/M operating system. To get the most from our discussions you'll need a functioning 128, a 1571 floppy disk drive, and a diskette with the CP/M operating system on it.

Turn on the computer, insert the diskette with the CP/M operating system in drive A and shut the drive's door. Pay attention to this sequence. If you turn the computer on or off with a diskette in the drive, a power surge from the read/write head could make your diskette unreadable—and unusable.

Now you've got your computer's power on and your CP/M system diskette in the drive. There are several methods to start CP/M on the Commodore 128. First, you could shut off the power, insert the CP/M system diskette and turn on the computer again. As mentioned above, this isn't the safest way. Another, much safer way is to turn the computer on, insert the diskette, and then press the RESET button.

The last way, which isn't much more complicated, is to insert the diskette and then enter the command:

`BOOT` <RETURN>

Pressing the RESET button is the usual method of entering CP/M mode, since it is the most dependable and fastest.

The disk drive will begin to read the diskette, its light will go on, and shortly thereafter you see a message on the screen. The start message looks somewhat different on every machine. That is because the message comes from the BIOS part of the operating system and varies from computer to computer. Before the Commodore start message comes on screen, you'll see the message `Booting...`, then in blue text, `Booting CP/M Plus`.

As you know, the Commodore 128 can use either a 40-column or an 80-column display. Its nice to work with an 80-column screen, but CP/M also supports a 40-column display. With the 40/80 display key you can choose between with the 40-or 80-column screen (providing you have the proper monitor). The initial message appears on either screen. After the CP/M prompt, only one display is active.

A 40-column screen simulates an 80-column display. By using <CONTROL> → and <CONTROL> ← you can shift the screen. Throughout this book, we assume that you are using an 80-column screen.

If you see the message:

```
NO CP/M+.SYS File - HIT RETURN TO RETRY

DEL TO ENTER C128 MODE
```

then you must have inserted the CP/M system diskette upside down. Turn the diskette over and press the <RETURN> key. Your Commodore will then boot CP/M.

There can also be disk read errors. In these cases, the screen displays the message:

```
READ ERROR - HIT RETURN TO RETRY
DEL TO ENTER C128 MODE
```

If you want to try to reboot, then press the <RETURN> key. If you're too frustrated to continue, press the <DEL> key. All other keys are ignored.

If everything goes as planned, first the following five lines will appear in the lower part of the screen:

```
BNKBIOS3 SPR F400 0800
BNKBIOS3 SPR CA00 1600
RESBDOS3 SPR EE00 0600
BNKBDOS3 SPR 9C00 2E00
58K TPA
```

These are information messages about the BIOS and BDOS, i.e., where they are stored and how long they are. This proceeds rapidly. `58K TPA` means that 58 KBytes of memory remain for programs and data. TPA means *Transient Program Area*. When these things are done, the following four lines appear on the upper part of the screen:

```
DATA TABLES
COMMON CODE
BANKED CODE
BIOS8502 CODE
```

When information from the diskette is loaded, the normal CP/M message appears on the screen. On the Commodore 128 it appears like this:

```
CP/M 3.0 On the Commodore 128 6 DEC 85

80 column display (or 40 column)
```

You've probably noticed that there are always some numbers in the lower right corner during loading. Even when the initial message disappears, these numbers don't go away. The last line of the screen is the *status line*, which can't be written on. The numbers in the corner show which block is being read from or written to. An `R` stands for reading from, and a `W` for writing to a block. Further down is an `A` or `B` message, indicating the disk drive that's being used.

The status line can be turned on and off with the key combination <CONTROL> <RUN/STOP> if you wish. *(80 column display only).*

What if you don't like the screen color? No problem. By hitting the <CONTROL> key and one of the keys 1 through 8, you can choose the display color. You can also change the background color by hitting the <CONTROL> key and one of the numerical keys 1 through 8 on the numerical pad. For example, if you want black print and a white background, press <CONTROL>-1 and <CONTROL>-2 (the latter combination from the numerical keypad). That's takes care of it. CP/M on the Commodore has other pleasant surprises waiting for you. *(80 column display only).*

Back to our start message again. The start message tells you that the CP/M operating system is stored correctly in the computer's work memory. Right after the start message display, CP/M puts up a ready message—the *operating system prompt*. The prompt looks like this:

```
A>
```

The large `A` tells you that you're working with disk drive A of your system. The > symbol is the ready message from CP/M. CP/M expects you to enter your command on the line with the prompt symbol. Well, then we won't make CP/M wait too long and we'll write:

```
A>abcdefgh
```

Now the cursor remains behind the last input character and doesn't move.

The reason is that CP/M doesn't know whether we've finished entering the command or if we still might have input. To have the input accepted, we must tell CP/M that we're done with the input.

We do this by pressing the <RETURN> or <ENTER> key. This is an abbreviation for *carriage return*, or *CR*. As soon as we press this key, the computer knows that a command has been given, and begins to carry it out. Press the <RETURN> key and the following appears:

```
A>abcdefgh
ABCDEFGH?
A>
```

What happened? CP/M read the line and did not find file `abcdefgh`, so it let us know. The operating system makes us aware of incorrect or uncomprehensible commands by repeating the input and followed by a question mark. The question mark means something like, "*What is this garbage?!? I can't do anything with it.*"

We'll try again—maybe the lowercase letters were the problem. After booting you can enter capital letters (using <SHIFT>). By hitting the <SHIFT LOCK> key you can enter capital letters every time. By the way, the key <C=> does exactly the same thing. Press the <SHIFT LOCK> key now.

```
A>ABCDEFGH
```

The following display comes back as an answer:

```
A>ABCDEFGH
ABCDEFGH?
A>
```

The operating system didn't understand the command in capital letters either. You might have wondered in the previous sample why the command line is repeated in capital letters, even though you entered lowercase letters. That is a quirk of CP/M that we need to pay attention to. CP/M converts all letters to capital letters and then interprets the input.

To show you that CP/M can really do something, we'll now enter a command that will really work. You read in a previous section that an entry on the diskette is managed by a table of contents. For this reason, CP/M puts a *directory* on every diskette.

To look at the table of contents, we enter the command `DIR`, which is an abbreviation for directory. Enter this command now and press <RETURN>:

`DIR` <RETURN>

A small note: As you may know, BASIC lets you see the table of contents on the screen by pressing the Function 3 key. Because the coding isn't too difficult, this is also possible in CP/M. Simply press the F3 key once. Pressing the F4 key displays the text `DIR` on the screen, without an automatic <RETURN>. We'll talk more about this option it later.

You'll see the directory of your operating system diskette on the screen. Take a closer look. On the far left of the directory listing, the drive identifier of the diskette is displayed. Next to this is the name of the data, separated from the drive name by blank spaces. You'll often see the abbreviation `COM`, for example, `CCP.COM`, `PIP.COM`, and `HELP.COM`. These names are explanations of their contents. Right now the `COM` programs are interesting to us because they contain usable programs.

`COM` is an abbreviation for *command*. These files contain commands which can be executed immediately. If you type in the name of one of these programs without the `COM` following the operating system prompt, the program will be put into the computer's memory and run. In other words, all you have to do is enter `PIP` and press <RETURN>. The program then begins to run.

2.6 Playing it safe

If you are still working with your original diskette, we'd like to suggest that you make a backup copy. You should get in the habit of making backups. It's a good idea to never work with the original program, but instead use a copy of the program and keep the original hidden away in a safe place. To make it easier to make backup copies, CP/M includes routines for the production of back up copies.

2.7 Summary

- You know a simple explanation of what an operating uses to manage its tasks.
- You know what a program is and why we use an operating system.
- You are familiar with CP/M's tasks.
- You know what the CP/M prompt is and how to look at the directory of your disks.
- You have learned that you should make at least one backup copy of every important diskette.

Chapter 3

Working with CP/M

Working with CP/M

3.1 The system diskette

You should always have backup copies of your original diskettes. If an accident destroys a copy, your originals will still be usable. Next we'll show you how to make a backup copy of the system diskette.

Two programs are needed to make backups. Type `DIR` <RETURN> to display the diskette's directory. You'll find two programs named:

`FORMAT.COM` and `PIP.COM`

Normally, a diskette containing the CP/M operating system is copied using the `COPYSYS` command. If you enter `COPYSYS` <RETURN> on the C-128 keyboard, you'll discover that it is inoperative. In other CP/M systems, `COPYSYS` copies the system tracks—tracks 0 and 1, which contain most of the CP/M operating system routines.

Under Commodore CP/M, the `FORMAT` command uses tracks 0 and 1. `FORMAT` places a `BOOT` sector on the diskette. Later, if the `RESET` button is pressed or the `BOOT` command is typed (in C-128 mode) when this diskette is in the drive, the CP/M system will be loaded automatically.

Unlike other CP/M systems, the programs on the system tracks are named. They are: `CPM+.SYS` and `CCP.COM`.

The file `CCP.COM` contains CP/M's *resident commands*. Resident commands are often-used commands that CP/M can perform without having to load `COM` files from diskette. The `CCP.COM` file is loaded during boot.

3.2 Copying with a single disk drive

Next we'll show you how to make a backup diskette if you have a single disk drive.

Insert your original CP/M systems diskette into drive A and close the door. Enter:

A>FORMAT <RETURN>

The following message is displayed on the screen:

```
C128 FORMAT PROGRAM
15 May 1985
Drive A is a 1571 (or 1541)

Please select disk type to format
C128 double sided
C128 single sided
C64 single sided
```

You can use the cursor keys (upper right of the keyboard) to select one of the three formats. Let's format a single-sided diskette. To do this, press the cursor down key (upper right) and press <RETURN>. The following appears on the screen:

```
Formatting C128 single sided

Insert diskette TO BE FORMATTED
in drive A. Type $ when ready,
any other key to abort
```

If you've changed your mind, press any key except the $ key to abort the program. Otherwise, press the $ key to continue. You'll see the following on the screen:

```
Formatting C128 single sided
```

If any error occurs, the screen is cleared, a warning message is displayed, and the disk drive's green LED light flashes (or red LED on the 1541). If this happens, examine the diskette. It may be damaged.

If there were no errors the following appears on the screen:

```
Do you want to format another disk?
```

Press the N key, since we only need a single formatted diskette for now. Remove the formatted diskette and reinsert the original system diskette.

Next copy the two system files: `CPM+.SYS` and `CCP.COM`. To do this, use the `PIP` command. As we will see later, `PIP` is a very useful program. For now, enter the following:

`PIP E:=A:CPM+.SYS` <RETURN>

The following message appears in the status line:

```
Insert Disk E in Drive A
```

Remove the original system diskette from the disk drive and insert the diskette we just formatted. Then press <RETURN>. The message disappears and the disk drive begins copying `CPM+.SYS` to the new diskette. When this is completed, the CP/M prompt reappears on the screen. Now copy `CCP.COM` in the same way:

```
PIP E:=A:CCP.COM
```

CP/M knows that you still have the destination diskette `E` in the drive. A message in the status line asks you to replace the diskette with the system diskette again. Do so and press <RETURN> again. When prompted, replace the system diskette with the `E` disk so that the data file `CCP.COM` can be copied. To display the table of contents of the new CP/M diskette, enter the command `DIR`. The status line requests that you insert the `A` diskette in the drive. Leave your diskette in the drive and press <RETURN> to change the `E` diskette the new `A` diskette.

That's all there is to it. The screen will display:

```
A: CPM+ SYS : CCP COM
```

This completes the first step. Since we want to make a copy of the entire diskette for backup, we need to copy all of the data files. To do this, enter the following command:

```
PIP E:=A:*.*
```

`PIP` tells you what file is being copied as it is working. A message in the status line requests you to change diskettes several times during the procedure. When you see this request, change the disks as instructed and press <RETURN>. When `PIP` is through, the entire first side of the CP/M system diskette will have been copied. The following files will be on it:

```
COPYING -
CPM+.SYS
CCP.COM
HELP.COM
HELP.HLP
KEYFIG.COM
KEYFIG.HLP
FORMAT.COM
PIP.COM
DIR.COM
COPYSYS.COM
```

To copy the second side (this is advised), format second diskette and enter:

```
PIP E:=A:*.*
```

Everything else is displayed on the screen as above. After you copy both sides, put the original system diskette in a safe place. If a copied diskette is destroyed, you will still have a backup for the CP/M system.

3.3 Copying with two disk drives

If you have two disk drives, you can copy data files much faster and more conveniently. You must first format a diskette. Make sure that the system diskette is in drive A and enter:

A>FORMAT <RETURN>

The following message is displayed on the screen:

```
C128 FORMAT PROGRAM
15 May 1985
Drive A is a 1571 (or 1541)

Please select disk type to format
C128 double sided
C128 single sided
C64 single sided
```

You can use the cursor keys in the first row of keys to select one of the three formats. Let's format a single-sided diskette. To do this, press the cursor down key (on the upper row of keys) and press <RETURN>. The following appears on the screen:

```
Formatting C128 single sided

Insert diskette TO BE FORMATTED
in drive A. Type $ when ready,
any other key to abort
```

If you've changed your mind, press any key except the $ key to abort the program. Otherwise, press the $ key to continue. You'll see the following on the screen:

Formatting C128 single sided

If any error occurs, the screen is cleared, a warning message is displayed, and the disk drive's green LED light flashes (or red LED on the 1541). If this happens, examine the diskette. It may be damaged.

If there were no errors the following appears on the screen:

```
Do you want to format another disk?
```

For now, press the N key, since we only need a single formatted diskette.

After the formatting is complete, replace the formatted diskette with the system diskette. Insert the formatted diskette into the B drive. Now enter:

`PIP B:=A:*.*` <RETURN>

The copying proceeds without any diskette change requests.

3.4 Displaying the directory

You have just copied data from drive A to drive B. To verify the contents of the diskette in drive B, enter:

```
DIR B:
```

Don't forget to insert a space after DIR. The command above tells CP/M to display the contents of the diskette in drive B. If you display the contents of an empty formatted diskette, the message NO FILE is displayed. This means that the diskette contains no data.

3.5 Copying with PIP

Usually PIP is used to copy data files with two-drive systems. But this command works differently on the Commodore 128. We can use a *virtual* disk drive by specifying drive E. This drive doesn't physically exist, but is recognized by the computer. Drive E physically uses drive A, by alternating diskettes. Before starting, you should note which diskette will be the A drive and which diskette will be the E drive. (This virtual memory trick works with more than just PIP, by the way. We'll talk more about its uses later).

The PIP program is an acronym for **P**eripheral **I**nterchange **P**rocessor, and can be a very useful program for us.

You have the system diskette in the disk drive at this time. Now type PIP and press <RETURN>. The computer loads the PIP program into memory. PIP displays its own prompt:

```
A>PIP
CP/M 3 PIP VERSION 3.0
*
```

The asterisk shows you that PIP is ready to accept commands. You'll get an in-depth look at the full range of PIP commands in Chapter 6.

Let's use PIP again. Here's our task: Copy the files from the diskette in drive A to the diskette in drive B (or drive E, if you only have one disk drive). An alternate way of saying this is: The diskette in drive B should receive the contents of the files contained on the diskette in drive A.

Why did we rephrase our goal for the task? Because PIP requires us to enter commands in a similar way. When the files on the diskette in drive A are copied to the diskette in drive B, both diskettes have identical contents. You'll notice that the commands contain an equal sign. Another way to state the command PIP B:=A:*.* is "make the contents of the diskette in drive B equal to the contents of the diskette in drive A."

The asterisk is a way to tell PIP to copy <u>all</u> files. You can think of the * as a wild card, which can be used to substitute for any card in any suit.

Recall that files are identified by a *name* and *extension*. The extension is a three letter identification following the period.

To copy all the data on a diskette, enter a `*.*`. It looks like this on the screen:

`B:=A:*.*` (or) `E:=A:*.*`

Because we want to make sure that all the data was transferred correctly, we can instruct it to do this as it is copying. This is done by placing a `V` in square brackets after the command, like this:

`B:=A:*.* [V].`

The `V` stands for Verify. By the way, the Commodore performs an automatic Verify, so the Option `[V]` command usually isn't necessary. But you should get into the habit of using it, so that if you switch to CP/M on a different computer model, you will have the same data verification.

As `PIP` is working, it displays the name of the file which it is copying. When work is completed, the `*` prompt is delayed. If there are no further commands, press <RETURN> and the familiar CP/M `A>` prompt is displayed.

3.6 Rules for filenames

You've run across the term *files* several times now, and you've seen filenames in the directories on your screen, but you still don't know what a file is, does, or what it's used for.

As you know, every file in CP/M has a name. That is important to you because it lets you see what is on a diskette. Unfortunately, CP/M's designers built in a few annoying limitations regarding filenames.

A *filename* in CP/M may have a maximum of eight characters, followed by a period, and then optionally followed by a three character extension to specify the data type. That means that filenames can use no more than eight characters, but must be descriptive enough to identify the file's contents.

Allowed characters for the filename are the 26 letters of the alphabet, numbers 0 through 9, and `+`, `-`, `/`, `%`, and `$` characters.

The following characters are not allowed in filenames or extensions, because they have special meaning in CP/M:

```
> > . , : = ; * ? [ ] !
```

Experience has taught us to always give a file a meaningful name. It's much harder to remember the contents of a file named `XK2512AC.ABC`, than `PAYROLL.DAT`.You can have two files on a diskette with the same filename, but different extensions, e.g. `PAYROLL.DAT` and `PAYROLL.CMD`.

3.7 Extensions

An extension is a three-character suffix that follows the filename. The idea behind an extension is to group similar files by type. Over time, users of CP/M systems have more or less standardized the extension names.

Programs that are ready to run by typing their name at the prompt (e.g. `A>`) have the extension of `COM`. You'll notice that `PIP`, `SYSGEN` and `COPYSYS` all have a `COM` extension.

Some programs make a copy of a file that may be modified. For example, if you are using the CP/M editor `ED` to modify a file called `TEXT.DAT`, it first creates a copy of that file with the extension `BAK` or `$$$`. `BAK` stands for *backup*. The data files with `$$$` extensions are temporary data files. They are used by a program and erased at the end of a program run. For example, `PIP` uses temporary data files and erases them completely from the diskette when its job is finished. Name your files to avoid confusing CP/M, as well as yourself.

If you use the same filename for more than one file and distinguish between them by using a different extension, then you should be aware of potential problems. Suppose you have two files named `TEXT.1` and `TEXT.2`. When you use `ED` to edit `TEXT.1`. it creates a copy of the original and remnames it `TEXT.BAK`. What happens if you now edit `TEXT.2`? When `ED` finds a file already named `TEXT.BAK`, it deletes it and thus destroys any backup copy of the original `TEXT.1`. Therefore you won't be able to use the original `TEXT.1` (now `TEXT.BAK`) file after editing `TEXT.2`.

To avoid this problem, you might name the first file `TEXT1.TXT`, the second one `TEXT2.TXT`, and the third `TEXT3.TXT`.

Then if you modify a file, a back-up copy is always created—you can always retrieve your original text if necessary.

3.8 Finding a data file

If you use your computer often, you'll probably create a lot of different files. This might make it difficult to locate files that you're looking for in the directory. It would be nice to be able to view files, for example, with names similar to `TEXT.TXT` that are contained on the diskette.

There are two different ways to search for these files.

The asterisk, you'll recall, is a wildcard. It can represent any string of characters.

The question mark is a wild card for a single character in a filename.

For example, the parameter `TEXT?` searches for all files with the name `TEXT` or with the name `TEXT` and one additional character. From the previous example, the files `TEXT1`, `TEXT2` and `TEXT3` would be found with the command:

`DIR TEXT?` <RETURN>

If a file named `TEXT` is also on the diskette, it too will be found and displayed. CP/M always reserves eight characters for a data filename. If you enter a filename with fewer than eight characters, CP/M fills in the rest of the positions with blank spaces. Therefore, blank spaces are as equally valid characters as are letters or digits.

3.9 Searching with a question mark (?)

Since the question mark can represent any character, then not only the files TEXT1, TEXT2 and TEXT3 will be found, but also the file TEXT. Entering a question mark doesn't let you delete a character, however. You can use as many as eight question marks when entering the file name and up to three question marks for the extension.

But this is wasted typing, since entering the beginning characters for a filename followed by an asterisk for the extension will do the same thing. The operating system doesn't distinguish between eight question marks and one asterisk. CP/M converts every asterisk into eight question marks before the search begins.

You can search using the asterisk more exactly if you put the first letter or letters of the desired data file in front of the asterisk. However, the search won't work if you enter an asterisk followed by letters. This method of inputting file names with question marks or stars, can be used with the commands DIR, TYPE, ERASE, SHOW, and PIP.

3.10 Summary

- You can now copy your system diskette and store your original in a safe place.
- You can simplify data file searches using asterisks and question marks in place of letters.
- You know that you should always use meaningful names for files.

Chapter 4

The resident commands

The resident (built-in) commands

In the last chapter we became acquainted with several of CP/M's basic commands. In this chapter we'll take a closer look at a number of *resident* CP/M commands: `USER`, `DIR`, `DIRS(YS)`, `ERA(SE)`, `REN(AME)`, and `TYPE`.

We'll also take another look at the *transient programs*. They are the CP/M programs that appear in the directory and are stored as `COM` data files. Finally, we'll expand on your knowledge of the `DIR` and `PIP` commands covered in Chapter 3.

4.1 Commands, parameters, and options

Let's take care of some preliminaries.

A *command* is a keyword that tells CP/M to perform a specific action.

A *parameter* is usually a filename that informs a command which file or data to use.

An *option* is a directive that changes the way the command functions. Options are specified in square brackets. An example of an option using PIP is the directive to verify the files as they are copied, `[V]`.

The number and type of parameters vary, depending on the particular command. If a parameter is required, but omitted, CP/M waits for you to enter it. It will not continue until you enter a parameter.

The command and parameters must be separated by at least one space. This is the only place where spaces are allowed. Spaces are not allowed within commands, parameters, or options.

If a parameter is too long to fit on a single line, you can use <CONTROL> E to continue entry on the following line. Commodore CP/M begins a new line on its own whenever this becomes necessary. CP/M reads the two lines as a single command line.

4.2 The resident commands

As previously mentioned, two types of commands are made available when CP/M is started.

Resident commands are loaded into memory from the file `CCP.COM`. Resident commands are built-in; that is, they are always in memory and ready for execution. To execute a resident command, type its *name*: `DIR` <RETURN>, and it will immediately start.

A *transient* command is not loaded into the computer's memory until it is needed. To execute a transient command, you also type its *name*: `PIP` <RETURN>, but it does not start immediately. Instead, it's loaded into the computer's memory from the system diskette and then started. Thus you'll notice a short delay as a transient command is read from diskette and then starts its execution.

CP/M 3.0 has six resident commands. They are listed below:

Command	Abbreviation	Function
DIR	DIR	Shows the contents of a disk
DIRSYS	DIRS	Shows the SYSTEM data files
ERASE	ERA	Erases files
RENAME	REN	Changes filenames
TYPE	TYP	Shows text files
USER	USE	Change's user range

You can execute a resident command by entering either the command or its abbreviation.

A seventh resident command doesn't have a name. This command allows you to switch from one drive to the other. To *log* onto drive B from drive A, type the following at the A> prompt:

A>**B:<RETURN>**

You can use drive designations from A to E. Any other designation causes the following error message:

```
CP/M Error On F: Invalid Drive
BDOS Function _ 14
```

If you're now using drive B and the system diskette is in drive A, you can still access programs from drive A. To do this, prefix the command with the drive designation like this:

B>**A:DIR**

You can also prefix a parameter with a drive designation:

B>**DIR A:DATEI.XXX**

4.3 USER and user areas

The USER command lets you divide an external storage media (floppy diskette or hard disk) into 16 *areas*. The areas are identified by numbers from 0 to 15. These areas are quite useful when several users are sharing a computer and and need to keep separate files, especially if the storage media is a hard disk. *User areas* make it easier to manage the large number of files that can be stored on the hard disk.

By specifying a separate user area for a particular purpose, you can better organize the data on the storage media. For example, in a classroom, each of 16 different students are assigned a unique user area. Or, you could designate one user area for text files, an area for your BASIC files, an area for your business letters, etc.

By dividing storage space into user areas, it's also possible to have two data files with exactly the same name and type identifier stored on the same storage device. Each data file goes into a separate user area.

4.3.1 USER areas in CP/M 3.0

User area 0 has a special function. Any programs and data files that are stored in user area 0 can be made available from any other user area, by making them SYS files. You might think of these files as *public* files. They can be made available to all users, like books at a public library. Files in other areas can be thought of as *private* files. They are available only to a specific user, like books in a private library.

When CP/M starts, you are automatically placed in user area 0. To change to a different user area issue the USER command:

USER 3 <RETURN>

and you're changed over to user area 3. Make sure that there is a space between USER and the number of the user area. You'll notice that the CP/M prompt changes. Instead of A>, the prompt now reads 3A> to let you know which area you are using.

Naturally you can use another disk drive. To log on to the B drive, just type:

3A> **B: <RETURN>**

and the prompt changes to 3B>.

Alternate methods of getting to this user area on drive B are:

A> **B3:**

(or)

A> **3B:**

If you are using both A and B drives, get back to the A drive:

3B> **A: <RETURN>**

If you display the directory now, the message NO FILE appears, since you haven't put any files into user area 3. CP/M separates the directory entries by user areas. This is helpful if many files in a single user area need to be displayed.

All of the built-in, resident commands are available from any user area.

4.4 DIR

We've already discussed the DIR command. Actually, there are two different versions of the DIR command: one is resident and the other is transient. If you enter DIR without any options (in square [] brackets), then the resident version is used. But if you do use options, then the transient version from the diskette (DIR.COM) is used.

The resident version displays the files on the diskette in the current user area . If you are logged on to user area 3, then only files stored in user area 3 are displayed.

Quite often, so many files are contained on a diskette that the directory doesn't fit on a single screen. You can pause the directory by pressing <CONTROL> S, continue the display by pressing <CONTROL> Q, or stop the directory by pressing <CONTROL> C.

If you are logged onto drive A but want to see if the contents of drive B, you can type:

A> **B:** <RETURN>
B> **DIR** <RETURN>

This logs you onto drive B and then displays the directory. Alternatively you can type:

A> **DIR B:**

This keeps you logged onto drive A., but displays the directory of drive B.

To get a hardcopy of the directory you can press <CONTROL> P before the DIR command. The <CONTROL> P turns on the printer hardcopy . Any information that is normally displayed on the screen is now redirected to the printer. Turn off the hardcopy by pressing <CONTROL> P again. This key combination is a toggle command, turning the hardcopy on and then off again.

4.4.1 DIR with parameters

You can also use parameters with the DIR command. If you have a large number of directory entries on a diskette, you can display the entry for a particular file, instead of reading through all the entries:

DIR B:TEXT.TXT <RETURN>

The filename is displayed if TEXT.TXT exists on the diskette in drive B. If the file is not on the diskette, the following is displayed:

```
No File
```

To use more complex functions of the DIR command, you must use the transient version. In this case, you must make sure that the file DIR.COM. is on the logged disk (usually on the A drive). For example, if the system diskette is in drive A, but you are logged onto drive B, you must issue the DIR command with options like this:

B> **A:DIR [*Options*]**

This ensures that DIR.COM is loaded from the A drive.

4.4.2 More about DIR

You'll recall that you can use asterisks in the DIR command. For example:

```
DIR *.COM
```

displays all of the *.COM files on the logged diskette.

You can also display the directory entries for several different file types:

```
DIR *.COM *.SYS
```

However, the above command will cause an error:

```
*.SYS?
```

Only the transient DIR command can handle this request.

To use the transient DIR command, do one of the following:

- prefix DIR with a drive identifier
  e.g. A: or B:

- append an option to the DIR command
  e.g. [FULL] or [DIR]

4.4.3 DIR and its options

Up to 18 different options are available to DIR. Normally you will won't use more than two of DIR's options at the same time. Options are always indicated by square brackets.

If more than one option is entered, they must be separated with commas or blank spaces. If the symbol of the option is unambiguous, you can abbreviate the option's name to two letters. You can also leave out the closing square bracket, but only if it's the last character on the command line.

For example:

```
DIR *.COM *.SYS [FULL]
DIR *.* [NOSORT,SIZE]
DIR *.BAS [USER=5 NOSORT SIZE
```

If the transient DIR is used, DIR.COM is loaded into the TPA. Remember that DIR.COM is about 15 KBytes in length and must be found in the directory before it is loaded. When it first starts, the screen displays:

```
Scanning Directory...
```

It then looks at the parameters and options. When this is done it begins to sort the filenames into alphabetical order (unless the NOSORT option is entered). DIR displays:

```
Sorting Directory...
```

Then the directory is displayed to the screen or the printer. A typical printout looks like this:

```
Directory for Drive A: User 0

  Name        Bytes  Recs  Attributes    Name        Bytes Recs Attributes
----------  ------  -----  -----------  ----------  ----  ----  ----------
CCP     COM    4k     25  Dir RW      COPYSYS COM   1k     3  Dir  RW
CPM+    SYS   23k    182  Dir RW      DIR     COM  15k   114  Dir  RW
FORMAT  COM    5k     35  Dir RW      HELP    COM   7k    56  Dir  RW
HELP    HLP   83k    664  Dir RW      KEYFIG  COM  10k    75  Dir  RW
KEYFIG  HLP    9k     72  Dir RW      PIP     COM   9k    68  Dir  RW

Total Bytes      =  166k  Total Records =  1296 Files Found =  10
Total 1k Blocks =  166  Used/Max Dir Entries for Drive A:  16/ 64
```

4.4.4 DIRSYS

When you display the directory, you may notice the following message:

`SYSTEM FILE(S) EXIST`

It tells you that, in addition to the files listed, the diskette also contains the *system files*. If you don't see the message, then no system files are contained on the diskette. System files are stored in user area 0, and can be read and used by every work area. If you'd like to display the names of the system files, enter the command `DIRSYS` or the abbreviation `DIRS`. Under the listed files you then receive the message that `No system files` exist.

You have the same capabilities with the command `DIRSYS` as with the command `DIR`. You can also use asterisks and question marks, as in the `DIR` command.

4.5 ERASE

The capacity of a diskette is limited, and therefore limits the number of entries on a diskette's directory. On a single-sided diskette, there is room for exactly 64 entries. On a double-sided diskette, the limit is 128 entries. If you use the transient DIR command, the maximum and current number of directory entries on the diskette is displayed.

When a file is no longer required, you will want to delete or erase it. This frees up space on the diskette so that it may be used by other programs. To do this you can use the ERASE command.

Enter the command like this:

ERASE *d*:*name*

The *d* represents the disk drive identifier. The *name* stands for the filename to be erased. If you are logged onto drive A and want to erase a file on drive A, then you can omit the drive identifier. The ERASE command can be abbreviated to ERA.

Like the DIR command, you can use asterisks and question marks with the ERA command. You should be very careful when using * or ? with ERA. It's easy to accidentally erase the wrong files and suffer the consequences afterwards.

To erase a specific type of file, for example, files with a BAK extension, enter:

```
ERA *.BAK
```

The following message is displayed:

```
ERASE *. BAK (Y/N)?
```

This is asking you to confirm the deletions. It's a safety precaution requiring you to respond before CP/M erases all of the files with the .BAK extension. Answer Y to delete the entries or N to abort.

If you are really brave, you can also erase all of the files on a diskette with this command:

```
ERA *.*
```

Once again you are asked to confirm the deletions:

```
ERASE *.* (Y/N)?
```

If you respond by typing a Y all of the files will be erased.

4.5.1 Erasing with ERA in CP/M 3.0

Suppose that you want to erase all .BAS files on a diskette. You would type:

```
ERA *.BAS
```

The following is displayed to make sure the files really should be erased:

```
ERASE *.BAS (Y/N)?
```

Before you answer Y for yes, you should double-check your typing. Are you certain that the command is correct and that you really want to erase this file type? Once you've typed a Y, there's no way to get the files back. The files are gone completely. Check especially for typing mistakes. For instance, it's easy to mistakenly type PAS instead of BAS. If you type in the command like this, all the Pascal files on your disk are erased.

To protect yourself against these unpleasant surprises, there are two ways to prevent accidental erasure. First, you can write-protect the individual files. You'll see how to do this shortly. Second, you can ask the ERASE command to confirm each deletion individually. To do this you must enter:

```
ERASE *.BAK[C]
```

Here, all files with the extension .BAK are erased, but only if you respond Y to the confirmation message.

4.6 Changing filenames with REN(AME)

To rename files, you use the RENAME command. The format looks like this:

RENAME *newname=d:oldname*

Note that *newname* precedes the *oldname* and that they are separated by the = sign. If the file *oldname* is on the logged drive, you can omit the drive identifier *d:*.

If the file *newname* already exists, you are asked if it should be erased before *oldname* is renamed to *newname*:

```
Error: Not renamed, newname file already exists,
                    delete (Y/N)?
```

If you answer this question with N, then RENAME is aborted.

If you enter Y, then the file newname will be erased, and the file oldname is renamed newname. It is interesting that the resident part of RENAME takes care of simple renaming, but if there are options—in this case, the new file already existed—then the transient RENAME is loaded before it continues. The abbreviation for RENAME is REN.

Here is an example of a "simple" renaming:

REN *new.bas=old.bas*

You can also use asterisks and question marks with the RENAME command. A simple example might look like this:

```
RENAME *.TXT=*.BAK
```

This command changes all the files with the extension TXT to files with the BAK extension. The RENAME command doesn't change the contents of a file, only its name.

4.7 TYPE

The `TYPE` command displays the contents of a file on the screen. It will display the contents of any text file that uses the ASCII character set. Other file types, for example `COM` or `REL` files, may contain characters that cause strange output or cause the computer to hang up. The format for the `TYPE` command is:

`TYPE` *d:filename*

To display the contents of a file from other than the logged drive, enter a different drive identifier.

The `TYPE` command displays 23 lines of text per screen. You can read the text on the screen an then press <RETURN> to view the next 23 lines of text. By entering the option `[NOPAGE]` the text is displayed in its entirety by scrolling continuously. You can halt the scrolling by pressing <CONTROL> S, and then restart the scrolling with <CONTROL> Q. Also, you can toggle <CONTROL> P to send the text to the printer.

The reverse side of the CP/M System diskette (the side titled `UTILITIES`) contains an assembler source file `DATE.ASM` that is a good example for using the `TYPE` command:

```
TYPE DATE.ASM
```

4.8 Summary

- CP/M has built-in commands that make it possible to work with and manipulate files on a disk.
- Commands can be entered with parameters or options.
- You know the names of all the built-in commands, how they work, and which options work only with the transient commands.

Chapter 5

The transient commands

The transient commands

5.1 Introduction

You have just read about CP/M's built-in, resident commands. But the real power of the operating system comes from transient commands. These are listed as COM files in the directory. We've noted several times that these commands are loaded into memory from diskettes when needed. These commands are stored on diskette for good reason: they are simply too big and would take up too much internal memory if they were built-in. Their size is due to the large number of options they give you.

Transient commands are first searched for in the directory and then loaded into memory. Therefore, they aren't as quickly accessible as their resident command counterparts. Keep this in mind when you work with CP/M.

5.2 Transient commands under CP/M

Now we'll take a look at important and often-used CP/M commands. Here we're referring to the transient commands found in the directory with COM extensions. You already know how to call the programs—type in the program name without the extension and press the <RETURN> key. There are three methods to call transient programs. First, you can work in user area 0. Second, you can make a program accessible to all user areas with a SET command. Third, you can use the SETDEF command. We'll talk more about this third command later.

5.3 SET

The `SET` command performs several tasks . Its main job is to set various file attributes. Attributes are special characteristics of a file. For example, you can use the `SET` command to make your CP/M files in user area 0 available to all user areas. Or you can protect a file by indicating, "*This file is read-only*" or "*This file is protected by a password.*"

The `SET` command also contains options which affect the table of contents (directory). For example, you can timestamp every file in the directory, to allow you to determine when the program was first created and when it was last accessed. You can use this timestamp later, to automatically back up all the files that were altered since a certain date to another diskette.

Here is an overview of the various options of the `SET` command:

<u>Option</u>	<u>Meaning</u>
`DIR`	Makes a system file visible to the normal directory.
`SYS`	Makes a file for `SYSTEM` file.
`RO`	Makes the file read-only.
`RW`	Makes a file read and write.
`ARCHIV=OFF`	Sets the `ARCHIV` attribute to off. That means that the file hasn't been backed up (put in an archive) yet. The program `PIP` can copy the files with the attribute `ARCHIV=OFF` by using option `AAU`. You enter the `PIP` command with asterisks for the filenames and `PIP` will copy all the files that have been changed since the last copying with `PIP` using option `AAU`. After `PIP` copies the files, it sets the file attribute to `ARCHIV=ON`.
`ARCHIV=ON`	Sets the `ARCHIV` attribute on. That means that this file has backed up. Normally `PIP`, using option `[A]`, changes the attribute after backing up the data. You can change the attribute yourself as well by using the `SET` command.

`F1=ON/OFF` Switches the user-defined file attribute F1 on or off.

`F2=ON/OFF` Switches the user-defined file attribute F2 on or off.

`F3=ON/OFF` Switches the user-defined file attribute F3 on or off.

`F4=ON/OFF` Switches the user-defined file attribute F4 on or off.

Let's see some examples of the `SET` command.

Suppose you have a program called `MYPROG.COM` that you want to be able to use from any user area. Normally this program is placed in user area 0.

An alternate way is to make your program a `SYSTEM` file. You can do this with the `SET` command:

```
SET MYPROG.COM [SYS]
```

You can also protect your program from being overwritten:

```
SET MYPROG.COM [RO]
```

Or you can make it a `SYSTEM` file and protect it:

```
SET MYPROG.COM [SYS RO]
```

To undo the attributes, you can enter:

```
SET MYPROG.COM [DIR RW]
```

The options may appear in any order (`[DIR RW]` or `[RW DIR]`) and may be separated by spaces or commas.

Note: To use the preceding commands, you should initialize the directory using the `INITDIR` command. You can prepare a diskette by typing:

```
INITDIR A:
```

This command reorganizes the directory of a diskette and prepares it for timestamping.

5.4 Disk drive characteristics

You can protect the contents of an entire disk drive so that information can only be read from it and can't be written to it. If you've set a disk drive to RO (read only), files can't be erased with ERASE, RENAME doesn't work, and PIP can't copy files to to that drive.

To do this, enter:

```
SET A:[RO]
```

Then, drive A is set to read-only. If you enter an RW (read/write) instead of RO, the drive can be written to again. Setting the read-only attribute does the same thing as putting on a write-protect tab.

5.5 Labels

You can give an entire diskette a name. A disk name is limited to eight characters, the same as for a filename. To do this you use the NAME= option of the SET command:

```
SET B:[NAME=FIBU]
```

If you have only one disk drive, the SET command will work if the file SET.COM is on the diskette being accessed. To get around this limitation, use the virtual disk drive E. Enter the following while the diskette containing SET.COM is in the drive:

```
SET E:[NAME=FIBU]
```

CP/M loads the required file SET.COM, and then asks you to insert the diskette representing drive E into the drive A. If you've entered the above command, the following text will appear on the screen:

```
Label  for  drive  E:

Directory      Passwds     Stamp      Stamp
Label           Reqd        Create    Update
---------      -------     -------    ------
E: FIBU   .    off         off        off
```

We'll talk about the other options marked `off` shortly.

The `DIR` command does not display a disk's name. To see the disk's name, use the `SHOW` command with the `LABEL` option:

```
SHOW E:[L]
```

When using one drive and the virtual drive `E`, CP/M repeatedly requests you to insert a disk into either the `E` or `A` drive. After you've responded to the request, press the disk `A` or disk `E` in the drive. Answer the request and then hit the <RETURN> key to proceed.

Now the output is more detailed than when we entered the `SET` command:

```
Label  for  drive  E:

Directory      Passwds     Stamp      Stamp
Label           Reqd        Create     Update  Label  created    Label  Updated
---------      -------     -------    ------  -------------    -------------
E:FIBU   .     off         off       off      12/06/85  01:04  12/06/85  01:04
```

Just like with more expensive computers, the creation date and the last time the file was updated are displayed. Whenever a file's contents are changed, the date of the update is also changed. Doing this gives us several advantages. For example, you can use the `PIP` command with a special option to update all the files that were changed on one particular day. But this is relevant only if you religiously enter the date and time using the `DATE` command whenever you work on the computer. Otherwise, the dates are inaccurate—like the ones in our example.

5.6 Diskette PASSWORD

Passwords can be used to prevent unauthorized access to data files. You can assign a password to an entire diskette and thereby restrict access to that diskette, as well as restrict the use of the SET command for the diskette.

Before assigning a password to a diskette, it must have a label (SET *d:* [*name=label*]). To assign a password enter:

SET *d*: [PASSWORD=*password*]

Now the diskette is password protected. If you try to use the SET command for this diskette the following is displayed:

```
Directory label
   Password?
```

Enter the correct password and press <RETURN> to gain access to the diskette. You'll notice that the password is not displayed on the screen as you're typing at the keyboard. This is an added security measure.

To remove a password from the diskette type:

```
SET [PASSWORD=<cr> (<cr> = <RETURN>)
```

Naturally you can remove the password only if you already know the password beforehand, since CP/M requires you to enter it here.

5.7 File PASSWORD

You can also assign a password to an individual file on a diskette. To assign file passwords you must allow the diskette to be protected:

SET *d*: [PROTECT=ON] <RETURN>

where *d* is the drive indicator for the diskette.

Now you can assign a password to an individual file. To assign the password SECRET to the file DIR.COM, type:

SET *d*:DIR.COM[PASSWORD=SECRET]<RETURN>

To remove a password from the file, enter:

SET *d*:DIR.COM[PASSWORD=off]<RETURN>

There are also several other options for protecting files:

READ The password is required to read, copy, write, erase, or rename a file

WRITE The password is required to write to, erase, or rename a file.

DELETE The password is required only to erase or rename a file.

NONE The password is removed

If you omit the option, READ is the default. Enter the option like this:

SET E:TEXT.TXT[PROTECT=DELETE]

This protects the file TEXT.TXT against accidental erasure.

To avoid confusion, we should understand that you cannot protect COM files in this way. If a COM file has has password with READ option, when you try to run this command you see this:

```
CP/M Error On A: Password Error
BDOS Function = 15 File = DIR .COM
```

You are not asked to enter the password before the command is run—the command is simply aborted.

When you want to remove a password, you are first asked to enter the password, which must be entered correctly. If you don't enter the password correctly, then you won't be able to remove it. This prevents unauthorized users from using these files.

5.8 Time Stamping

A time stamp is similar to punch-clock in a factory that records each employee's working hours by the date and time. CP/M can timestamp files. The timestamp can then be used to determine the last time a file was accessed or updated, for example.

Three steps are required to use timestamping:

`DATE`	command to set the date and time
`INITDIR`	command to prepare a diskette's directory to record the timestamp
`SET`	command to turn on the timestamping

To set the date and time enter:

`DATE SET` <RETURN>

The DATE command displays:

```
Enter today's date (MM/DD/YY):
```

Enter the date in the format `month/day/year` including the slash between numbers and press the <RETURN> key. Next the `DATE` command displays:

```
Enter the time (HH:MM:SS):
```

Enter the current time in the format `hour:minutes:seconds` including the colon between numbers and press <RETURN>.

You can verify your entries by entering:

`DATE` <RETURN>

This displays the date and time. These values are updated as long as the computer's power remains on.

Next you must initialize the diskette to accept the timestamps. Here we use the `INITDIR` command. We recommend that you first make a backup copy of the diskette. Since the `INITDIR` reorganizes the diskette's directory, if it should encounter any errors, the data on the diskette may become inaccessible. This is why we recommend making a backup. To initialize the diskette for timestamping, enter:

`INITDIR` *d*: <RETURN>

The `INITDIR` command displays the following:

```
INITDIR WILL ACTIVATE TIMESTAMPS FOR SPECIFIED DRIVE
Do you want to re-format the directory on drive:d (Y/N)?
```

Press Y and <RETURN> to reorganize the directory.

Now you can use the `SET` command to begin recording the timestamps. There are three options available:

`CREATE=ON` records the time stamp only when a file is created.

`ACCESS=ON` records the time stamp when a file is read.

`UPDATE=ON` records the time stamp when a file is changed.

`CREATE` and `UPDATE` are mutually exclusive. You can also turn off the time stamp by using `OFF` in place of `ON`.This is because when you change a file, you make a new file. The old file becomes a BAK (backup) copy.

To record the current date and time, you enter the following command:

```
SET E:[ACCESS=ON]
```

To see the result of this command, enter:

```
DIR[FULL]
```

The following directory will be displayed:

```
Directory for Drive B:

  Name      Bytes   Recs  Attributes    Prot  Update    Access

   TEXT.TXT  5K       38   DIR   RW     NONE              04/01/85 17:31
   FIBU      20K     152   SYS   RO     NONE              04/01/85 09:10
```

The ACCESS option lets you find out when you last accessed a file. The command for two entries in the table of contents looks like this:

```
SET E:[CREATE=ON,UPDATE=ON]
```

This directory is then displayed:

```
Directory for Drive B:

Name      Bytes Recs Attributes Prot  Update             Create

TEXT.TXT   5K     38  DIR   RW   NONE  04/17/85:10:00   01/01/85 09:00
FIBU      20K    152  SYS   RO   NONE  04/17/85:16:43   01/01/82 19:21
```

5.9 SETDEF

After CP/M receives a command, it always looks for the specified file on the disk drive currently in use—indicated by the the drive designator displayed onscreen. The SETDEF command lets you alter this. For example, if you are working with drive B but have all your CP/M files stored on drive A, SETDEF will allow you to tell CP/M the search path to use. In this way you can store and retrieve programs from the correct disk dirve automatically, without having to specify the drive designator every time.

If you enter:

SETDEF <RETURN>

you'll receive information about the current search path, which disk drive is used for temporary files, and what type of file is being sought. It looks like this on the screen:

```
Drive Search Path:

1st Drive               - Default

Search Order            - COM
Temporary Drive         - Default
Console Page Mode       - On
Program Name Display    - Off
```

You can change the search path with the following command:

```
SETDEF A:
```

This command instructs CP/M to search for and retrieve the desired files on drive A only, even if you are presently working on drive B. You can expand the command like this:

```
SETDEF A:,*
```

CP/M then first looks for the files on drive A, and then on the drive currently in use (represented by the asterisk). Each time you enter a SETDEF command, you get an information list as follows:.

```
Drive Search Path:
1st Drive              - A:
2nd Drive              - Default
```

You can have this information sent to the printer with <CONTROL> P.

If you want temporary files (like the ones PIP uses) to be written to a specified drive, enter:

```
SETDEF [TEMPORARY=E:]
```

This command will write temporary files to the virtual drive E. CP/M recognizes the temporary files because their $$$ file extensions, as discussed previously.

SETDEF normally only searches for files with a COM or SUB extension. By default, CP/M searches for COM files first, but this order can be changed with the following command:

```
SETDEF [ORDER=(SUB,COM)]
```

This changes the search order so that SUB files are sought first. SUB files are called with the SUBMIT command, and contain a batch of runable commands. We'll discuss the SUBMIT command in detail shortly.

5.10 SHOW

The SHOW command can give you a lot of information about your disks: the amount of space on your disks, the names of your disks, and the number of files per USER. When you enter:

```
SHOW
```

you'll see the status of all of the disk drives, as well as the remaining space on each drive. Obviously, the utilities disk must be present in the drive.

```
A: RW, Space: 11k
E: RW, Space: 2k
```

If you enter the drive designator behind it, you only get information for the disk in the specified drive.

The SHOW command also lets you see the labels on your disk:

```
SHOW A:[LABEL]
```

You can abbreviate LABEL to L. On the screen you will see the following table of contents:

```
Label for drive A:

Directory   Passwds   Stamp   Stamp
Label       Reqd      Create  Update  Label Created    Label Updated

FIBU.COM    off       off     off     04/17/85 11:41   04/17/85 11:41
```

Another option of the SHOW command lets you see which USER areas on your disk are being used, and how many files are in each area. Enter this option as follows:

```
SHOW A:[USER]
```

The command will display the number of free entries in a table of contents:

```
A: Active User : 0
A: Active Files: 0 2 11 12
A: # of files : 22 6  1 1

A: Number of free directory entries:   24
```

If you simply enter:

```
SHOW A:[DIR]
```

you'll just be shown the number of free directory entries—you get the last line of the previous screen display.

The `SHOW` command is closely related to the CP/M 2.2 command `STAT`. CP/M 3.0 features several new commands that are derived from the single CP/M 2.2 `STAT` command. Therefore, the `SHOW` command is more powerful and user-friendly than its predecessor, and has none of its limitations.

5.11 SUBMIT

You've learned to enter CP/M commands through the keyboard. By now you've probably noticed that you have to type in the same commands and same instructions over and over again. This redundant input can get quite annoying. CP/M has a command to relieve you of this burden.

The SUBMIT command lets you store a "batch" of often-used commands and the '128 will treat them like keyboard input. A SUBMIT file has the extension SUB.

The SUBMIT command can make repetiitve CP/M tasks much easier. For example, the '128 doesn't have a built-in clock. Consequently, you have to enter the time and date every time you boot up the computer. If you want to require an up-to-date time stamp on every file access, you can make use of the file PROFILE.SUB. This file will be accessed and run after every boot or restart. The file's commands will be used as a SUBMIT file. PROFILE.SUB is comparable to the AUTOEXEC.BAT files on the IBM PC and compatibles.

If you decide that the time and date should be entered, you don't enter it in the usual way. You write the file like this:

```
A:DATE SET
```

and name this file PROFILE.SUB. (You can also enter another disk drive, providing it contains the DATE.COM file). Don't forget the SUB extension.

If you want to enter a file through the keyboard, you can use the editor ED. Since ED is quite difficult to use, there is still another possibility: by using the PIP commands. You can enter files through the keyboard with the PIP command, but cannot edit them:

```
PIP PROFILE.SUB=CON:
```

Wait until the disk drive stops running. Enter the line of text above (A:DATE SET) and then hit <RETURN>. If you want to enter several lines, continue to make entries. You must enter <CONTROL> Z as the last line.

A SUB file holds many possibilities. It can contain CP/M commands, interlocked SUBMIT commands, or input programs or CP/M commands.

You can also use parameters in a SUB file. These parameters are represented by dollar signs ($). You can use the parameters $1 through $9.

For example, enter the following lines:

```
ERA $1.BAK
DIR *.$2
```

Name this file DIR.SUB. The set of commands in this file first erase all files with a particular name and with the extension .BAK. Then it displays all the files with a particular extension. To run the file, you enter:

```
SUBMIT DIR TEXT COM
```

Here DIR is the name of the SUBMIT file, and TEXT and COM replace the parameters $1 and $2. When the file is run, first all the files with a BAK or $1 extension are erased. Then all the files with a COM extension are displayed (provided the SUBMIT.COM file and the SUB file are on the same disk side: otherwise the virtual drive E must be used). The "translated" SUBMIT file—the submit files with its inputted parameters—looks like this:

```
ERA TEXT.BAK
DIR *.COM
```

CP/M uses these commands as if they were entered through the keyboard.

If you enter fewer parameters than there are in the SUBMIT file, those parameters won't be used. If you enter more parameters than the SUBMIT file contains, the extraeneous parameters are ignored. If you want to use a dollar sign in a command inside a SUBMIT file, enter two dollar signs ($$).

A SUBMIT file can also execute command input for programs. You can call a program with one command line and use the next to enter commands to the called program. For example:

```
PIP
<B:=A:*.COM
<
DIR *.COM
```

This small SUBMIT file calls PIP.COM in the first line. The second line is the command to copy all the COM files to drive B. The third line exits PIP, and the fourth displays the directory. All commands to be entered into a program are identified with a less than sign (<). If you enter a command without additional parameters, as with the third line, it signifies a <RETURN>, which in this case ends PIP.

The SUBMIT command can be quite useful. For example, you can execute a series of files and go get something to eat while they run. You write the command file like this:

```
PIP LST:=FILE1
PIP LST:=FILE2
PIP LST:=FILE3
.
.
.
PIP LST:=FILE9
```

You can accomplish the same thing with the following command line:

```
PIP LST:=FILE?
```

Name the file BUNCH.SUB and enter the following before you leave:

SUBMIT BUNCH.SUB <RETURN>

You can also store the individual files on different disk drives. You need only write the drive designator in front of the filename and SUBMIT searches for all the files concurrently.

You could write a command file to list all the data files in all the USER areas on a hard disk drive. The screen output can then be written to a new file with the name Contents. In this file you can look for a specified file with a search command in your text program, or print the file list.

5.12 The HELP command

By this time, you're probably having trouble remembering all of the many CP/M commands, not to mention all their options. Fortunately CP/M contains a help program to remind you of all the command codes and their options. You need only tell CP/M where you need help.

Simply enter the command HELP:

```
A:>HELP
```

A menu with the possible help information packages is displayed on the screen. There you choose a subpoint and will receive information about it.

Incidentally, the Commodore 128's keyboard features a <HELP> key that normally displays a program error in the BASIC operating system. Under CP/M, pressing this key displays the word HELP onscreen, without an automatic <RETURN>. This allows you to enter a word after it when you know which topic you need assistance with.

The following is displayed the screen when you enter HELP without specifying a topic:

```
HELP UTILITY V1.1

AT "HELP>" enter topic [,subtopic]...

EXAMPLE: HELP> DIR EXAMPLES

Topics available:


C128_MODE COMMANDS CNTRLCHARS COPYSYS      DATE      DEVICE
DIR       DUMP     ED         ERASE        FILESPEC  GENCOM
GET       HELP     HEXCOM     INITDIR      KEYFIG    LIB
LINK      MAC      PATCH      PIP (COPY)   PUT       RENAME
RMAC      SAVE     SET        SETDEF       SHOW      SID
SUBMIT    TYPE     USER       XREF
HELP>
```

You can also enter the subtopics directly. For example, you can enter:

```
HELP SETDEF
```

This displays help information on SETDEF directly.

The HELP program is contained in the file HELP.COM and HELP.HLP. To alter these files, call the file HELP.COM and enter the EXTRACT option:

```
HELP [EXTRACT]
```

The following display will appear on the screen:

```
Extracting Data...Extraction complete
HELP.DAT Created
```

You can abbreviate the EXTRACT to an E. The HELP program then creates a new file with the name HELP.DAT. You can change this file as you see fit using your text editor. By using the EXTRACT option you set it up so that you can edit the topics.

To enter new help text, you must follow certain format rules. Every option word must begin with three slashes (///) and a number. The number gives the help steps of the option. For example:

```
///1DIR <RETURN>
///2OPTIONS <RETURN>
///3PARAMETERS <RETURN>
///4EXAMPLES <RETURN>
```

Once you've made your changes, store the data and call HELP.COM again, but this time with CREATE option (abbreviated C). This creates a new HELP.HLP file that contains your text alterations.

5.13 Summary

- You've learned about the transient commands of CP/M
- You know the options that change or expand the tasks of the transient commands
- You know that files can be given labels
- You've seen how we can protect an entire disk, a file, or an individual CP/M command for restricted use
- You know how to prepare a time stamp for your files that furnishes the time and date of when a file was last accessed.
- You know how to alter the file search path with `SETDEF`
- You know how to display the system files of a disk using `SHOW`
- You can use the `PROFILE.SUB` file to make your computer's boot routine automatically run a program

Chapter 6

Everything about PIP

Everything about PIP

You've already heard about some of the capabilities of PIP. Here is a complete list of its capabilities:

- Transfer a single file from one diskette to another
- Transfer a group of files from one diskette to another
- Copy a file and rename it
- Format text for printing
- Shorten lines of text in a file
- Print a group of files
- Merge several files into one
- Access a section of a text file
- Change lowercase letters to uppercase letters and vice versa
- Reset the eighth or flag bit of a byte to zero
- Insert line numbers into a file
- Display a file during transfer
- Transfer system files
- Copy files from one user area to another
- Automatically back up new or altered files

As you can see, there are many uses for PIP. You might do well to read this chapter thoroughly so that you may use PIP to your greatest advantage.

6.1 Diskette copying

Nearly every programming book advises you to make a copy of any original diskette for backup purposes. We saw how to do this earlier. Let's look at a simple example. To copy a file called `TEXT.TXT` from the diskette in drive `A` to the one in drive `B`, enter:

```
A>PIP <RETURN>
*B:TEXT.TXT=A:TEXT.TXT <RETURN>
```

By doing this, you copy the file `TEXT.TXT` from the diskette in drive `A` to drive `B` and give it the same name. The original file in drive `A` remains unaltered.

To copy the complete contents of a diskette, enter:

```
A>PIP <RETURN>
*B:=A:*.* <RETURN>
```

This transfers all of the files from drive A to drive B. If you have only one disk drive, you can copy all the files to the virtual drive `E` using the command:

```
A> PIP E:=A:*.* <RETURN>
```

This procedure involves more work for you, since you must alternate the diskettes in the single disk drive. But without it, you wouldn't be able to copy files with a single drive.

There are a large number of options that may be used with the `PIP` command. One option is `[V]`, for verify. As `PIP` copies a file with the verify option, the copy is checked to make sure that the data was transferred correctly. Enter the command like this:

```
A>PIP <RETURN>
*B:=A:TEXT.TXT[V] <RETURN>
```

If you prefer, you can enter the parameters and options on the same line as the command, like this:

```
A> PIP B:=A:TEXT.TXT[V] <RETURN>
```

Using this method, PIP immediately begins copying; when it has finished, it displays the prompt (A>). You probably noticed that we didn't enter a filename for drive B. The filename defaults to the same name as the file being copied. To change the filename when you copy, enter:

```
PIP B:TEXT1.TXT=A:TEXT.TXT
```

This lets you copy a file and change its name at the same time.

Before copying files to another diskette, you should make sure that there is enough space on that diskette for the new file.

PIP transfers each file to a temporary file that has the same filename, but with the extension $$$. As each file is successfully transferred, PIP renames the temporary file with the specified filename.

What happens when you try to copy a file to a diskette that already has that particular filename—for example, TEXT.TXT ? First, PIP transfers the file to a temporary file called TEXT.$$$. Next the old version of the file TEXT.TXT on the destination diskette is erased. Finally TEXT.$$$ is renamed TEXT.TXT. If the destination diskette doesn't have enough space for the new file, then you will have to erase the old TEXT.TXT file first.

As you transfer files using PIP without special options, the file attributes such as SYS, DIR, RO, and RW are also transferred. If you transfer a SYSTEM file, the copy will also be a SYSTEM file.

If you transfer a file to a destination diskette that has the same filename and is write-protected (RO), PIP asks you to confirm that it should erase this file. Respond with either Y or N as appropriate.

6.2 Copying between USER areas

Unless you specify otherwise, `PIP` copies files only within the same user area. If you are in `USER` area 3, `PIP` copies are transferred to `USER` area 3 on the destination diskette.

To transfer files from one `USER` area to another, you must specify the `[G`*n*`]` option, where *n* is the number of the new `USER` area. To transfer `TEXT.TXT` from `USER` area 0 on drive `A` to `USER` area 2 on drive `B`, enter:

```
PIP B:[G2]=A:TEXT.TXT
```

This command assumes that you are logged onto `USER` area 0 when you enter the command.

6.3 Text files and non-text files

As far as `PIP` is concerned, it can differentiate between two types of files: *text* files and the *non-text* files.

A text file is usually created by an editor such as `ED` or a wordprocessor. A text file is stored as a series of readable characters.

The end of a text file is indicated by a <CONTROL> Z character. As a result, any text following the <CONTROL> Z character in a text file is ignored.

Non-text files may contain any characters, not just readable ones. Therefore a non-text file may contain imbedded control characters like <CONTROL> Z. With non-text files, `PIP` does not recognize <CONTROL> Z to be the end-of-file indicator.

6.4 Merging data files

If you want to merge the contents of two or more files into a single file, you can do this with PIP. Normally these files must be text files. Merging COM files produces a non-executible program.

To merge (or concatenate) files using PIP, the filenames to be combined are separated by commas:

```
PIP ALL.TXT=PART1.TXT,PART2.TXT,PART3.TXT
```

This assumes that all of the files are contained on the same drive. If the file is to be merged into a different USER area, enter:

```
PIP ALL.TXT[G3]=PART1.TXT,PART2.TXT,PART3.TXT
```

And to assure that the files are verified as they are merged, include the [V] option:

```
PIP ALL.TXT[G3]=PART1.TXT[V],PART2.TXT[V],PART3.TXT[V]
```

If you try to merge non-text files, you may encounter problems. PIP understands the <CONTROL> Z character as the end-of-file character. Non-text files may contain <CONTROL> Z characters.

If you use PIP to transfer a COM file, then a <CONTROL> Z character is transferred normally; it is not an end-of-file indicator. Instead, PIP continues to copy until the actual end-of-file.

To copy files that are neither text files nor COM files, use the [O] option following the filename:

```
PIP ALL.DAT=P1.DAT[O],P2.DAT[O]
```

6.5 Line numbering

PIP can also insert line numbers into a text file. This feature is often used by programmers or writers who want to identify their lines of text by number. If you copy a file using the N options, a line number is inserted at the beginning of each line of text:

```
PIP TEXTNR.TXT=TEXT.TXT[N]
```

The text now appears like this:

```
1: This is your text
2: numbered by line.
3: Practical, isn't it?
```

You can also insert a six digit line number by using the N2 option:

```
PIP TEXTNR.TXT=TEXT.TXT[N2]
```

The text now appears like this:

```
000001 This is your text
000002 numbered by line using option N2.
000003 Also practical, isn't it?
```

The line numbers are assigned sequentially and the order can't be changed.

6.6 Converting between uppercase and lowercase

To convert the text of a file to all uppercase, you can use the [U] option:

```
PIP CON:=TEXT.TXT[U]
```

To convert the text of a file to all lowercase, you can use the [L] option:

```
PIP CON:=TEXT.TXT[L]
```

6.7 Searching for a string

If you're printing a text file with `PIP` and the paper in the printer jams up, you may not want to print 200 pages again. You can restart the operation using the `[S]` option of `PIP`. To display the file `TEXT.TXT` beginning at the word *hungry*, enter:

```
PIP CON:=TEXT.TXT[S hungry<CONTROL> Z]
```

The search string is ended with <CONTROL> Z. You can also use the `[Q]` option to end the transfer when a search string is formed:

```
PIP COM:=TEXT.TXT[Q people<CONTROL> Z]
```

You can of course combine `[S]` and `[Q]` in a single transfer:

```
PIP CON:=TEXT.TXT[S hungry<CONTROL>Z Q people<CONTROL>Z]
```

If the search string is not contained in the source file, one of the following error messages appears:

```
ERROR: START NOT FOUND
```

(or)

```
ERROR: QUIT NOT FOUND
```

6.8 Printing data files

We already talked about toggling the printer to get hardcopy. By pressing <CONTROL> P, screen output is sent to the printer. To print a file you could do the following:

<CONTROL> P	toggle printer on
`TYPE TEXT.TXT`	list file
<CONTROL> P	toggle printer off

An alternate way to do this is to use the `PIP` option to transfer the file to the printer. The printer is designated by the `LST:` device, so you can enter:

```
PIP LST:=TEXT.TXT
```

Of course, you can also print multiple files one after the other:

```
PIP LST:=TEXT1.TXT,TEXT2.TXT,TEXT3.TXT
```

Other options are available to insert line numbers, set TABs, and eject a new page every 60 lines. We'll see these options later.

6.9 Automatically backing up data files

As you use CP/M, you'll find yourself creating and modifying many different files. Then, in case one of the files is accidentally (or deliberately) destroyed, you will still have a backup copy of your data.

CP/M has a method to help you organize your backup copies.

Each file has what is called an *archive flag*. A file's archive flag indicates if a backup has been made using PIP. When a file is created or updated, its archive flag is set to 1. When a backup is made, the flag is reset to 0.

Usually backups are time-consuming, because copies are made of each file. You can save time by using the [A] option of PIP, which copies a file only if the file is new or is changed—that is, if the file's archive flag is 1.

To make a backup copy of the new or changed TXT files, enter::

```
PIP B:=A:*.TXT[A]
```

This copies any TXT files to the diskette in drive B if the archive flag is 1.

You'll probably want to insure that the copies are transferred without error, so you can use the [V] option:

```
PIP B:=A:*.TXT[AV]
```

If you display the directory of the diskette in drive A using:

```
DIR[FULL]
```

then the keyword arcv appears under the attributes indicating which files were backed up.

6.10 Overwriting without prompts

Normally `PIP` overwrites a file on a destination diskette if the filename is the same as the one that is being transferred. But if the file on the destination diskette is protected by the `RO` attribute (`SET` command), then the following message appears:

```
DESTINATION FILE IS R/O, DELETE (Y/N)?
```

You can overwrite the file by pressing Y, or abort the operation by pressing N.

To avoid having to respond to this prompt, you can use the `[W]` option of `PIP`. For example:

```
SET TEXT.TXT[RO]
PIP TEXT.TXT=NEW.TXT[W]
```

will allow the file `TEXT.TXT` to be overwritten, even though it has been previously set to read only.

6.11 Copying system data files

PIP normally cannot copy a file with the SYStem attribute. By using the [R] option, PIP is able to find the SYSTEM file. To copy a diskette with SYSTEM files enter:

```
PIP B:=A:*.COM[R]
```

To determine if system files are contained on a diskette, use the DIRSYS command.

6.12 Tidying up the 8th bit

ASCII characters can be coded in seven bits of an eight-bit byte. The eighth bit is unused.

Some programs such as WordStar® use the eighth bit for special purposes. Other programs require the eighth bit to remain unused—for example, MBASIC®, the BASIC interpreter for CP/M. If you use WordStar document mode to edit a MBASIC program, the program will not run correctly, since WordStar uses the eighth bit. You can fix this problem using PIP's [Z] option:

```
PIP NEWPROG.BAS=BADPROG.BAS[Z]
```

This "strips" any used eighth bits from the file BADPROG.BAS as it transfers the contents to NEWPROG.BAS.

6.13 Practical examples

In this final section of this chapter, we'll cover a few examples using PIP in various "real-life" applications. You've gotten to know various PIP options and also learned that you can use them together.

To get hardcopy you can enter:

```
PIP LST:TEXT.TXT[NT8P60]
```

The file TEXT.TXT is printed to the LST: device. Each line is numbered [N], the tabs are set at column 8 [T8], and each page will contain a maximum of 60 lines of text [P60].

To display the text in lowercase, enter:

```
PIP LST:TXT.TXT[NT8P60L]
```

Here we've added the [L] option to do this.

Suppose you want to back up files on a daily basis. To do this you enter:

```
PIP A:=B:*.*[WAR]
```

The option [WAR] works as follows: the [R] option copies the SYSTEM files, the [W] option overwrites any read only files, and the [A] option copies only files that have not been previously copied.

You can create a submit file (let's call it ARCHIVE.SUB) containing the above command. A SUBMIT file is a text file containing one or more commands. Then we can enter the command:

```
SUBMIT ARCHIVE
```

This takes the text from the file ARCHIVE.SUB and performs the commands as if they were entered at the keyboard. To create ARCHIVE.SUB, enter:

```
A>PIP <RETURN>
*ARCHIVE.SUB=CON: <RETURN>
PIP A:=B:*.*[WAR] <CONTROL> Z
```

Next you can SUBMIT this file. This will transfer the files that have not been backed up from the B drive to the A drive.

You can also enter:

```
SUBMIT ARCHIVE[E]
```

and the commands contained in the SUBMIT file are echoed to the screen.

Naturally you can put other commands such as DIR and SHOW in the SUBMIT file. This lets you see which files and how many files are copied, as well as the amount of space contained on the destination diskette.

The 128 has several more device designations than other CP/M systems have, because of its 40- and 80-character screens. These designations are as follow:

KEYS	keyboard of the Commodore 128
40COL	40 character screen
80COL	80 character screen
PRT1	serial printer (device number 4)
PRT2	serial printer (device number 5)

The following notations for input and output are available:

CONIN:	KEYS
CONOUT:	80COL (40COL)
AUXIN:	Null Device
AUXOUT:	Null Device
LST:	PRT1

Note that the standard printer output is to a serial printer, which has the device address 4.

6.14 Summary

- `PIP` is one of the most powerful CP/M utilities
- You can transfer a single file to another diskette
- You can copy an entire diskette onto another
- You can merge several files into one
- You can extract a section of a file
- You can automatically number the lines of a text file
- You can automatically back up altered files
- You can convert uppercase letters into lowercase letters and vice versa
- You can copy between `USER` areas

Chapter 7

CP/M components

7.1 CP/M on the C-128

CP/M 3.0 is supposed to be identical for all computers, yet there are often unique features of the hardware and architecture of the machines require special adaptations of the CP/M functions.

One of the most obvious differences between the 128's CP/M 3.0 and others is that their system diskette is special. This diskette can be read by either the 1541 or 1571 disk drive. One drawback of this arrangement is that the 1571 is not able to access both sides of the diskette without the user removing it and flipping it over to its other side. `COM` files are located on both sides of the diskette, yet they may be accessed only in the 1571's one-sided mode. More about the 1571 next.

7.2 System diskette for 1571

To take advantage of the 1571's greater storage capacity you need to do a little extra preparation. First of all, you must format a diskette as double-sided. Type:

```
FORMAT
```

The following appears on the screen:

```
Please select disk type to format
C128 double sided
C128 single sided
C64 single sided
```

Use the cursor keys on the upper row of the keyboard to select `C128 double sided` and press the <RETURN> key. Then insert a <u>blank</u> diskette into the drive. Press the $ key only when you are sure that it is safe to format the diskette in the drive.

After this is done, you will copy both sides of the original system diskette to the new system diskette. Place the original with the label "128 CP/M SYSTEM DISKETTE" in drive A and type:

	`PIPE:=A:*.*`	if you have one drive
(or)	`PIP B:=A:*.*`	if you have two drives

If you are using one drive, you are asked to change diskettes several times. Follow these instructions, keeping in mind that the destination diskette E is the newly formatted one.

After the first side of the original has been copied, you must copy the second side. To do this, insert the original system diskette into the drive with the label facing down and enter:

```
     PIP A:=E:*.*   if you have one drive
(or) PIP B:=:E:*.*  if you have two drives
```

After you finish, you will have a double-sided system diskette. Use this diskette with your 1571 and take advantage of the greater storage capacity and convenience of a double-sided disk.

7.3 Virtual disk drive E

By design, the C-128 allows you to use up to four disk drives. In 128 mode, these are assigned device numbers 8, 9, 10 and 11. Under CP/M these devices have the identifiers `A:`, `B:`, `C:`, and `D:`, respectively.

You've already been introduced to drive `E` in Chapter 3. But what is a *virtual* drive? Virtual refers to something which appears to exist, but really doesn't. The fifth drive may be addressed, but doesn't really exist except in internal memory. The data on drive `E` resides in memory until it is copied to a physical diskette in drive `A`. CP/M differentiates between drive `A` and drive `E` and knows if it is to address the real drive `A` or pretend to address virtual drive `E`. It alternates between drive `A` and drive `E` by prompting you to change diskettes when necessary.

By using the virtual drive, you can use `PIP` to copy files even though you only have a single real drive. If you have two disk drives, you have a great advantage over those users with only one. For instance, copying is much faster, and you can access much more storage capacity at one time. By all means make full use of this second (or even third or fourth) disk drive. But even if you have these advantages, sometimes it's faster and easier to use the virtual drive.

7.4 The COPYSYS command

With other CP/M computers, the operating system programs are located on tracks 0 and 1, and are copied with the COPYSYS command. On the C-128, the operating system is contained in the files named CPM+.SYS and CCP.COM. You can copy these to another diskette using PIP.If you run the COPYSYS command, you will see that this command is not available for the '128. Instead, you should do the following to copy the system programs to a new diskette in drive E:

```
FORMAT
PIP E:=A:CPM+.SYS
PIP E:=A:CCP.COM
```

After FORMATing and PIPing the system files, you will be able to start (boot) CP/M with the new diskette. Since it doesn't contain any transient commands, copy the COM files from the original to the new system diskette.

7.5 The status line

The last line on the screen is called the *status line*. The information here are messages that CP/M displays. For example, when using the virtual drive, CP/M displays a prompt on the status line asking you to insert the `A` diskette or `E` diskette.

Disk information is displayed in the lower righthand corner of the screen. The format of the information is as follows:

```
O Dtt ss
```

The symbols used above have the following meanings:

- `O` = Operation: (R)ead or (W)rite
- `D` = Drive being accessed (A, B, C, or D)
- `tt` = two-digit track number / track presently being read or written
- `ss` = two-digit sector number / sector presently being read or written

The display changes as the disk operation changes.

Track and sector numbers are separated by a space. If the diskette has been formatted in the MFM-format (a double-sided disk) and you are accessing the second side, the track and sector displays are separated by a dash (-).

If you do not want to display this disk status, you can turn it off (80-column only) by pressing <CONTROL> <RUN/STOP>. The <CONTROL> key must be held down while pressing <RUN/STOP>. To reactivate the display, simply press the same key combination.

You cannot display your own messages on the status line. This is reserved for use by CP/M.

You can echo the last command that you manually typed at the keyboard by pressing the ↓ (cursor-down) key on the bottom row. The separate cursor block on the upper right of the keyboard will be excluded here, because it has another important function. For instance, if you have entered the `DIR*.*` command and pressed <RETURN>, you can press the cursor-down key and the command will be redisplayed below—but without the <RETURN>. This is so you can make any necessary changes in the command before it is executed.

7.6 1571 disk formats

The 1571 disk drive is capable of reading various diskette formats.

The 1571's controller can be programmed to read and write different formats, unlike the earlier 1541 drives. You can use the following diskette formats with the 1571 drive:

Osborne DD	(1024 bytes/sector, single sided, 5 sectors/track)
Epson QX10	(512 bytes/sector, double sided, 10 sectors/track)
IBM-8 SS (CP/M 86)	(512 bytes/sector, single sided, 8 sectors/track)
IBM-8 DS (CP/M 86)	(512 bytes/sector, double sided, 8 sectors/track)
KayPro II	(512 bytes/sector, single sided, 10 sectors/track)
KayPro IV	(512 bytes/sector, double sided, 10 sectors/track)

Thus six different formats are directly supported.

As you've probably noticed, the drive motor spins shortly after you insert the disk and close the door. The disk drive is attempting to identify the format of the disk. To do this, the drive checks bytes per sector, and sectors per track. If this isn't sufficient to identify the format, a small box in the lower left-hand corner of the screen shows the possible formats. You may then select the correct format by scrolling through the list of choices. Use the ← or → (cursor left and cursor right keys) to view the choices.

When you have scrolled to the desired format, confirm the selection by pressing <RETURN>. If you wish to use that format exclusively, hold the <CONTROL> key while pressing <RETURN>. This way CP/M knows which format is being used, and will not ask you to enter the correct one each time you switch diskettes.

7.7 The keyboard

The 128 keyboard functions differently under CP/M than in 64 or 128 mode.

For example,the cursor keys do not work the same as they do when using BASIC. Pressing the cursor down key on the bottom row of the keyboard redisplays the command last entered. But the cursor down key on the top row of the keyboard has no effect.

You can re-boot the CP/M system from the keyboard by pressing <CONTROL> <ENTER>. Note that the <ENTER> key is part of the numerical keypad.

Each key on the 128 may have up to four different values. A key's value may be: unshifted, shifted, control, and caps lock. The shifted value is not always the same as the caps lock value. When you enter an unshifted value, make sure that the caps lock key is in the "up" position. The characters appearing on the screen should then be lowercase. The <40/80 DISPLAY> key has no effect on the key values.

A shifted value is produced by holding the <SHIFT> key and pressing the desired key.

A control value is produced by holding the <CONTROL> and pressing the desired key.

To enter the "simulated" caps lock mode, press the Commodore key (C=). In this mode, only letters will be shifted. Numbers and other characters remain unshifted in "simulated" caps lock mode.

Using an 80-column monitor, you can change the background and cursor color. To change the cursor color, press a number keys on the top row of the keyboard in combination with the <CONTROL> key. The cursor will change color correspondingly. To change the background color, press a number key on the numerical keypad in combination with the <CONTROL> key. These colors correspond to the colors used in BASIC.

7.8 Keyboard values

The 128's keyboard is very flexible under CP/M. You can essentially assign a new value to each key.

We've already noted that CP/M uses the ASCII character set. These characters have values from 0 to 127. Any value greater than 128 ($80) in hexadecimal has a different use—it may set the colors of the screen display or substitute a predefined string of characters. Here's a list of these values:

`80-9F`	predefined strings 0-15
`A0-AF`	80-character foreground colors
`B0-BF`	80-character background colors
`C0-CF`	40-character foreground colors
`D0-DF`	40-character background colors
`E0-EF`	40-character border color
`F0-FF`	special functions

7.8.1 Disabling/enabling 80 column color selection

You can change the foreground color on a 80-column color monitor with <CONTROL> *<top row number>* combination. You can also change the background color with the <CONTROL> *<numerical keypad number>* combination. When you press one of these key combinations, a value of 160-167 or 176-183 is produced that changes either the screen's foreground or background color.

To disable this color selection, you can press the following key combination:

<CONTROL> <RSHIFT> <ALT>

<RSHIFT> is the right <SHIFT> key. You must use the right <SHIFT> key and not the left one. All three keys must be pressed simultaneously to disable the color selection.

After pressing this key combination, you cannot change the screen's foreground or background color with <CONTROL> *<top row number>* or <CONTROL> *<numerical keypad number>*.

You can re-enable the foreground/background color selection by entering the <CONTROL> <RSHIFT> <ALT> combination again. This key combination acts as a toggle. Press the combination once and it disables. Press the combination again and it enables.

If you disable the color selection, the <HELP> is also disabled.

7.8.2 Changing a key's ASCII value

When you press a key or a combination of keys (such as <SHIFT> <A> or <CONTROL> <C>), CP/M encodes the key's physical location on the keyboard to a numerical value ranging from 0 to 255 ($00 to $FF hexadecimal).

For example, when you press the space bar, CP/M recognizes that the long key on the bottom row of the keyboard was depressed. CP/M associates this key with a value of 32 ($20 hexadecimal).

Under CP/M on the '128, you can change the encoding of each key. Using what we'll call the *keyboard editor*, you can change CP/M so that pressing the space bar produces the value normally associated with the letter "A" (65=$41).

To use the keyboard editor, enter:

<CONTROL> <RSHIFT>< ←>

The key denoted as < ←> is the cursor left key on the top row of the keyboard.

Next press the key whose value you want to change. For example, press the space bar. A highlighted area on the status line appears:

20

The value 20 is a hexadecimal number and represents the space bar's current value. This value is what we normally expect to see, since a space has an ASCII value of 32 ($20 in hexadecimal). To change the space bar so that it will produce the value for the letter "A", enter a new value: `41`. The highlighted area will disappear from the status line. You have now exited the keyboard editor.

Now let's try out the key board to see if the change was effected. Press the space bar. The letter `A` will appear on the screen at the cursor. This isn't a very useful change, since you now have no way of entering a space. Enter the keyboard editor again and undo the change. Press:

<CONTROL> <RSHIFT> <←>

Now the current value of the space bar is displayed:

```
41 20
```

Change the value back to its original value 20 and the keyboard is back to normal.

As you have noticed, all values are displayed and entered in hexadecimal notation. See **APPENDIX A** for a complete list of the characters and their values in hexadecimal notation.

Changing the space bar to produce the letter "A" wasn't very useful. Let's try another example that will be of more use to us. Recall that a key value greater than 127 has a different use than the ASCII values. On a 80-column color monitor, you can normally change the background to one of eight different colors. Actually, it is possible to select from 16 different colors. Each different background color is represented by a value from $B0 to $BF (or $D0 to $DF for 40-column screens).

To select the first eight colors, you press <CONTROL> *<number>*, where *<number>* is a number on the numerical keypad. For example, the key combination <CONTROL> <1> produces the value $B0 and changes the background color to black. But we are limited to eight colors with the <CONTROL> key combination.

We can use the keyboard editor to be able to select the other eight colors. If we decide to use the <SHIFT> *<number>* key combination, and assign these to values between $B8 and $BF, then the other eight background colors are available.

Enter the keyboard editor:

<CONTROL> <RSHIFT> <←>

Now press <CONTROL> <1>, keeping in mind that <1> is on the numerical keypad. The following is displayed:

```
D1
```

Change this key combination's value to `B8`. You have now added the background color selection for the <SHIFT> <1> key combination. You can add the other seven background colors similarly.

7.8.3 Defining the function keys

If you press a function key, a text string appears on the screen. By default, the function keys are assigned the following string values:

F1	F 1	
F2	F 2	
F3	`dir`<CR>	
F4	`dir`	
F5	F 5	
F6	F 6	
F7	`F7`	
F8:	6 Dec 85	(may differ on your system)

Pressing <F1> produces the value $80, <F2> produces $81, and so on. Pressing <HELP> produces $9F. As CP/M recognizes a keyboard value from $80 to $9F, it substitutes a string.

For example, when you press <HELP>, the value $9F is produced, in which CP/M substitutes the text "Help." You can redefine the text associated with each of the values $80 to $9F by using the *function key editor*.

To use the function key editor, enter:

<CONTROL> <RSHIFT> < →>

where < →> denotes the cursor right key on the top row of the keyboard.

A highlighted area appears on the status line of the screen. Now press the key <HELP>, or <F1> to <F8>, whichever key you wish to change the text of. For this example press the <HELP> key, and the following appears on the status line:

```
>Help<
```

The symbols > and < are the start and end of the text. A block cursor is positioned over the first character of the string `H`. For now, don't press any of the keys. We'll first explain explain the purpose of some of the keys.

Key combination	Function
<CONTROL><RSHIFT> < → >	move cursor right
<CONTROL> <RSHIFT> < ← >	move cursor left
<CONTROL> <RSHIFT> < + >	insert space at cursor
<CONTROL> <RSHIFT> < − >	delete character at cursor
<CONTROL> <RSHIFT> <RETURN>	end function key editor

To change the text of the <HELP> key to "`dir a:`", simply type the letters and the screen will look like this:

```
>dir a:<
```

If you press <RETURN> without holding <CONTROL> <RSHIFT>, a carriage return is inserted into the text (it appears as a lowercase `m`). Then exit the function key editor with the key combination:

<CONTROL> <RSHIFT> < RETURN>

Now every time you press the <HELP> key, you will display the directory of the `A` drive. You'll notice that you can assign text strings to any value form $80 to $9F. Therefore you can define up to 32 different text strings. To invoke these strings you will have to use the *keyboard editor* (discussed in the previous section) to assign one of these values to the desired key.

For example, some printers aren't able to print the symbol £. You could substitute the string "`Pounds sterling`" for the symbol. To do this, first change the key value of the £ key from its normal value $23 to one in the range $80 to $9F. Let's change it to $99.

Do this by using the keyboard editor:

<CONTROL> <RSHIFT> < ←>

and pressing the `£` key. You'll see the following on the status line:

```
23
```

Enter the new value `99`. Now you can edit the text string that is associated with "pseudo function key" `£`. Press the following:

<CONTROL> <RSHIFT> < →>

and then press the `£` key. You will see:

```
>     <
```

Type the words "`Pounds sterling`" and then press:

<CONTROL> <RSHIFT> < RETURN>

The highlighted area in the status line disappears as it accepts the new text string. Now if you press the £ key, the words `Pounds sterling` appear. You've successfully programmed a new function key!

Here is a complete list of the functions and their hexadecimal codes:

$80	F 1	$90	F17
$81	F 2	$91	F18
$82	dir<CR>	$92	F19
$83	dir	$93	F20
$84	F 5	$94	F21
$85	F 6	$95	F22
$86	F7	$96	F23
$87	6 Dec 85	$97	F24
$88	F9	$98	F25
$89	F10	$99	F26
$8A	F11	$9A	F27
$8B	Screen left	$9B	F28
$8C	Screen right	$9C	F29
$8D	Screen left	$9D	F30
$8E	Screen right	$9E	F31
$8F	F16	$9F	HELP

From the table above, it appears that the text strings for codes $8B to $8E or omitted. Actually, these codes are used to scroll the 40-column screen horizontally.

In the following table, the values $FO to $FF are reserved for *special functions*. These special functions, which are defined for the 128's CP/M, are as follow:

`$F0`	turn disk status on/off
`$F1`	pause/unpause display
`$F2`	40-column
`$F3`	left screen (40-column)
`$F4`	right screen (40-column)
`$F5`	MFM unlock
`$FF`	reboot system

To invoke code $F0, press <CONTROL> <RUN/STOP>. This causes the disk status line to disappear.

To invoke code $F1, press the <NO SCROLL> key. Pressing it once temporarily halts the display of information on the screen and displays PAUSE on the status line. Pressing it a second time reactivates the display.

To invoke code $FF, press <CONTROL> <ENTER>. This is the equivalent to turning the computer off and then on again.

7.9 `KEYFIG` functions and uses

Both the keyboard editor and function editor described in the previous section are *resident*. You may use either at any time. However, if you frequently change key values or "program" the function keys, you'll soon realize that these are time-consuming tasks.

There's another way to change the key values and program the function keys—by using the `KEYFIG` transient command.

Make sure the system diskette is in the logged drive and enter `KEYFIG` <RETURN>. The following will appear on the screen:

```
C128 SOFT KEYBOARD PROGRAM

3 Jan 1986

Welcome to the Commodore C128 Keyboard
Definition program. Do you want help?
```

You should never refuse an offer for help, especially if you are using a command for the first time. Enter `Y` for Yes to display the following menu:

```
Help is available on the following topics:
 -->done help<--
 -->General Usage<--
 -->Setting up your work file<--
 -->What to do with your work file<--
 -->Key values<--
 -->Selecting a key to edit<--
 -->Logical/Physical colors<--
 -->Editing keys<--
 -->Assigning/Editing strings<--
 -->Assigning colors<--
 -->Assigning special functions<--
 -->Assigning hex values<--
 -->Finishing up<--
 -->For experts only<--

 Use the up and down arrow keys to scroll
 through the menu; type the <RETURN> key
 to select the topic on which you want help.
```

Many of the headings are self-explanatory, but even so you may want to read each of them, in order to gain a better understanding of `KEYFIG`. Select the desired function by scrolling up and down with the cursor up and cursor down keys (↑ and ↓ on the top row of the keyboard).

To confirm the selected function (highlighted), press <RETURN>. The option `-->For experts only<--` will tell you that the <CONTROL> <RSHIFT> combination is considerably faster. Once you have had enough help, select `-->done help<--`, and `KEYFIG` will continue.

If you want to make changes in your keyboard layout (i.e., define function keys, simulate foreign keyboards, etc.), you'll need a way of saving these definitions, to avoid having to make the changes over and over again. `KEYFIG` can save the changes permanently. After you exit the >Help< mode, the following display appears on the screen:

```
From which of the following sources of
key definitions would you like to work?

    Default definitions
    Definitions on the CP/M boot disk
    Current definitions
    (Your previous work file)
```

Choose the set of key definitions you want to work with by using the cursor keys. The option in parenthesis will not appear if you are booting CP/M for the first time. Depending on the option you choose, the system will or will not retrieve the new keyboard definition from the diskette. The third line indicates which keyboard definitions are being used.

To find out how easy it is to use `KEYFIG`, choose the second option when the following menu is displayed:

```
Edit a key definition
Set up logical<-->physical colors
Exit and save your work file
```

If you are using an 80-column color monitor, the pallette of colors are displayed. These colors represent logical (key-defined) and physical colors. You may rearrange this list of colors by simply entering their correspondingly letters. The changes are displayed immediately.

To change the key definitions, choose the option `Edit a key definition`.The following menu appears:

```
                 Editing:   no key
```

This key has the 4 values shown below:

```
          normal→
          CMDR SHFT→
          SHIFT →
          CTRL →
  (done editing-exit and save work file)
```

Here too, you select the desired option by using the cursor keys on the top row. If a key is pressed, its four values appear on the screen. `CMDR SHFT` on the screen display (<C=> <SHIFT>) is equivalent to <CAPS LOCK>. (Remember, the <CAPS LOCK> key is inoperative under CP/M).

One of the impressive features of `KEYFIG` is its ability to describe in text what it cannot display. For example, it can describe the left-arrow located in the upper lefthand corner of the keyboard as `LEFT ARROW NEXT TO 1`. Thus a key like <DELETE>, for which an ASCII code can't be displayed, is described in text. For example, the text for the <DELETE> key is `RUBOUT`. If you wish to change one of the four definitions per key, move the marker to that option and press <RETURN>.

```
ASSIGN a STRING (more than 1 character)
ASSIGN new (single) character
ASSIGN a COLOR
ASSIGN hex value
ASSIGN a SPECIAL FUNCTION
don't modify this key
```

`KEYFIG` allows you to save these modifications. You may save the changes on the system diskette or a separate diskette. If the changes are saved on the system diskette, they are loaded automatically when CP/M is rebooted.

To save your keyboard changes, select the following options:

```
Exit and save your work file
on CP/M boot disk
```

After the changes are saved, KEYFIG will ask:

```
Do you want to do anything else []
```

Answer Y or N as appropriate. To exit KEYFIG at any time, you can press <CONTROL> C. KEYFIG asks you to confirm this so that you don't exit the command accidentally.

Chapter 8

Additional utilities

Additional utilities

In this chapter we'll take a look at several utilities. These utilities are part of the CP/M development package available from Digital Research.

If you're a beginning CP/M user, you might want to skip this chapter. In fact, this chapter might be renamed "CP/M for Advanced Programmers".

The CP/M development package includes an assembler, disassembler, monitor, and other utilities for the CP/M machine language programmer.

We'll take a look at some of these utilities shortly.

8.1 The assemblers MAC and RMAC

MAC and RMAC are both assembler programs. They are successors to the original ASM assembler distributed by Digital Research.

MAC is a *macro assembler*. RMAC is a variation of MAC that generates relocatable object code. Relocatable code is machine code that can be executed from any location in the computer's memory.

The three assemblers do their work in 8080 code. Two LIB files containing several macros are included with the development package.

One LIB file is called Z80.LIB and the other X6502.LIB. Using these LIB files, you can assemble Z-80 mnemonics with MAC and RMAC, although most of the opcodes still look like 8080 mnemonics. For example, the LD HL,0 instruction must be coded as LXI H 0. Additional Z-80 instructions are added to the 8080 instructions—examples are relative jumps, the IX and IY registers, and the exchange register instructions.

You can list these mnemonics by entering:

```
TYPE Z80.LIB
```

You can program in 6502 machine language using the other macro library.

The development package actually contains two assemblers. Let's look at the MAC assembler first. First a little background. The 8080 processor is the predecessor to the Z-80 contained in the '128, and in a certain sense is its "parent." The Z-80 can execute programs that the 8080 understands, but has a larger vocabulary (or instruction set) and different *mnemonics*. Mnemonics are the notations for the machine language instructions used in writing assembly language programs.

As you know, a machine language consists of a line of binary numbers. For example, the Z-80 processor understands the instruction $41 and can execute it. But it's very difficult for a human to associate this number with any particular instruction or function. Mnemonics are used to represent these machine codes and make them easier to understand. With the Z-80, the mnemonic for the instruction $41 looks like this:

```
LD B,C
```

This mnemonic has a specific meaning to the machine language programmer. It makes programming much easier, because you don't have to keep referring a table to find out what code `$41` does.

But the processor can't do anything with the mnemonic `LD B,C`. The assembler's task is to convert these mnemonics, which humans understand, to codes that the computer can understand. The assembler acts as a sort of interpreter, translating the human language into machine language. The `MAC` assembler also supports the user in other ways, which we'll mention later.

We've mentioned that the older 8080 processor is the parent of the Z-80. You also know that the Z-80 has more instructions that the 8080. This is important to know, since *all* CP/M programs must be written in 8080 code.

This is because there are many CP/M computers equipped with the earlier 8080 processor. Consequently, a Z-80 programmer is limited to those commands that the 8080 can understand. This precludes some quite useful Z-80 instructions.

On the Z-80, the code `$41` represents the following mnemonic:

```
LD B,C
```

On the 8080, this same code represents this mnemonic:

```
MOV B,C
```

Either represents the same operation: transfer the contents of the C-register to the B-register. The operations are identical; the notations are different.

8.2 Using the MAC assembler

One of the problems you'll encounter in machine language programming is in referencing memory locations when performing instructions like loading or saving a register. Another common problem is keeping track of memory location jumps. For instance, suppose you write a program that starts at memory address $5000, and later want to move it to address $4000. You'd have to change all jump addresses (except for the relative jumps) within the program. If you insert a new instruction into a program, all of the relative jumps and all other jumps are shifted. It would be nerve-wracking to try to keep track of all these addresses.

To make this work easier, the MAC assembler allows us to define *labels*. Labels are transformed into actual memory addresses during the assembly. With labels, it's no longer a problem to insert a new instruction at or to move a routine to a different memory location—the assembler does all the work for you.

The MAC and RMAC assemblers allow you do this and much more. The "Additional Utilities" diskette contains these programs. Insert it into drive A. List the directory:

```
A: LIB       COM : LINK     COM : MAC        COM : RMAC     COM : SID COM
A: CBDOS3    SPR : BNKDOS3  SPR : CRESBDOS3  SPR : HEXCOM   COM : XREFCOM
A: CALLVERS  ASM : DUMP     COM : ZECHOVERS  ASM : RANDOM   ASM : HISTUTL
A: TRACE     UTL : READ     ME
```

Notice the file named DUMP.COM. The syntax for this command is:

DUMP *<filename>*

DUMP displays the contents of the specified file in hexadecimal format (hex dump). To see a sample DUMP display, enter:

DUMP DATE.COM

The file contents of DUMP.COM is displayed on the screen. You can pause the scrolling output by pressing <CONTROL> S and start it again with <CONTROL> Q. Alternatively, you can use the <NO SCROLL> key, which you might find more practical. You can terminate the output by pressing <CONTROL> C.

DUMP.ASM is the assembly language source program for the DUMP command. You can display the ASCII contents of this file on the screen (or printer) if you wish. Enter:

```
TYPE DUMP.ASM
```

The program header is the Digital Research copyright notice (the original developers of the CP/M operating system).

Here is a small example of what appears on the screen when you DUMP a COM file:

```
00A0 00 C9 3A 13 02 FE 80 C2 B3 01 CD CE 01 B7 CA B3
00B0 01 37 C9 5F 16 00 3C 32 13 02 21 80 00 19 7E B7
00C0 C9 AF 32 7C 00 11 5C 00 0E 0F CD 05 00 C9 E5 D5
00D0 C5 11 5C 00 0E 14 CD 05 00 C1 D1 E1 C9 46 49 4C
00E0 45 20 44 55 4D 50 20 56 45 52 53 49 4F 4E 20 31
00F0 2E 34 24 0D 0A 4E 4F 20 49 4E 50 55 54 20 46 49
0100 4C 45 20 50 52 45 53 45 4E 54 20 4F 4E 20 44 49
```

Now here's a short example of an assembler listing:

```
update$clock:
        mov     a,c
        cpi     11              ; console status function?
        jnz     next            ; no, then just exit
                                ; yes, update the time
        lxi     h,0
        dad     sp
        shld    ret$stack
        lxi     sp,local$stack
```

This is a good comparison of the assembly language source program (.ASM) and the hexadecimal machine language display (.COM). It's obvious that the assembly language source is much more readable. You can even insert comments into the assembly language source to describe the program. These comments start with a semicolon so that the assembler knows it should ignore these lines of text. Otherwise the assembler would try to assemble them, and cause numerous errors in the process.

The DUMP.ASM program may appear to be very long, but it's actually quite short for an assembly language source code listing. Consider that the operating system is written in assembly language—when printed out it can reach a full 2000 pages in length. Even programs like the word processor TEXTOMAT can easily reach 400 to 500 pages.

As you can see, programming in machine language can be a very time-consuming process. Our goal here is to assemble a program to demonstrate the operation of the assembler.

Copy DUMP.ASM to your the backup copy of the Additional Utilities diskette. Make sure that your diskette is not write-protected, since we have to write to the diskette on which the source code is located. You have made a backup-copy of your CP/M diskette, haven't you? (If not, do so quickly). To assemble this source program, enter:

```
MAC DUMP
```

Notice that you don't have to specify the filename extension. You don't have to type DUMP.ASM, because the assembler automatically appends the extension .ASM. The following display appears on the screen:

```
CP/M MACRO ASSEM 2.0
0257
002H USE FACTOR
END OF ASSEMBLY

A>
```

The assembler quickly creates three files:

- An assembler listing named DUMP.PRN
- A hexadecimal file called DUMP.HEX
- A symbol table named DUMP.SYM

Take a look first at the assembler listing by entering:

```
TYPE DUMP.PRN <RETURN>
```

Here's an illustration of what should appear on your screen:

```
0112 11F301   LXI      D,OPNMSG
0115 CD9C01   CALL     ERR
0118 C35101   JMP      FINIS     ;TO RETURN
                                 ;OPENOK:
                                 ;OPEN OPERATION OK,
                                 ;SET BUFFER INDEX TO END
011B 3E80     MVI     A,80H
011D 321302   TA      IBP        ;SET BUFFER POINTER TO 80H
                                 ;HL CONTAINS NEXT ADDRESS TO PRINT
0120 210000   LXI      H,0       ;START WITH 0000
```

The assembly language program is listed with all of the information added by the assembler. The first column lists the address at which the code is located—if a label is defined, the first column contains the value of the label. The program starts at address $0100 and ends at $0257. As a result we know the meaning of the number the assembler printed (see above). Most CP/M programs begin at address $0100.

After reviewing the assembler listing, or printed out a hardcopy, look at the second file created by the assembler. Enter the following:

TYPE DUMP.HEX <RETURN>

Her's an illustration of what should appear on your screen:

```
:100130004401CD7201CD59010FDA51017CCD8F01FF
:100140007DCD8F01233E20CD650178CD8F01C32366
:1001500001CD72012A1502F9C9E5D5C50E0BCD05F1
:1001600000C1D1E1C9E5D5C50E025FCD0500C1D101
:10017000E1C93E0DCD65013E0ACD6501C9E60FFE20
:100180000AD28901C630C38B01C637CD6501C9F5D6
```

A set of numbers is displayed. These are the program codes (opcodes). Other information is displayed, such as the address to which the code will later be moved. This file is already considerably shorter than the DUMP.PRN file. There is also a symbol table with the extension .SYM.

But we still can't execute this machine language program, since it isn't a COM file. There is another program called HEXCOM that creates a COM file from a HEX file. To do this enter:

HEXCOM DUMP

Notice that an extension is not entered. `HEXCOM` automatically adds the extension `.HEX`. The screen then displays:

```
HEXCOM VERS: 3.00

FIRST ADDRESS 0100
LAST ADDRESS 0212
BYTES READ 0113
RECORDS WRITTEN 03
```

You have just created a `COM` file, the file `DUMP.COM`. We can execute `DUMP.COM` by simply entering:

`DUMP DUMP.COM` (displays itself)

Next we'll discuss a few things about the assembler, so that you can use it properly. The source programs for the assembler are ASCII text files. Each line of text has the following format:

<line number><label> : *<mnemonic><argument>* ; *<comment>*

The *<line number>* is optional. It need not be present, as in our example. It is ignored by the assembler, and used here only because some text editors (such as `ED`) automatically insert line numbers. The *<mnemonic>*: is also optional, but if used must be placed at this location. The *<mnemonic>* and the *<argument>* must be included in all assembler source lines, unless the line is a line of comments.

The assembler converts lowercase letters to uppercase before processing them. This simplifies programming greatly. The one exception to this rule is the letters between quotation marks representing a fixed string—these letters are left in lowercase, as in the following instruction:

```
DB "File Dump Version 1.4"
```

The individual components of an assembler source line are separated by at least one space. It is standard practice to begin the line with the *<label>* (far left) and then use the editor to TAB to the next components. This is not required, but it improves the readability of the program. The program listing will be in neat columns, like in this example:

```
DISKR:      ;READ DISK FILE RECORD
             PUSH H! PUSH D! PUSH B
             LXI  D,FCB
             MVI  C,READF
             CALL BDOS
             POP B! POP D! POP H

             RET
```

The above program segment is from the `DUMP` program. `DISKR` is a label, and labels are always identified by a colon. Then comes the mnemonic and the argument, in that order.

You also see another feature of the assembler in this short routine. Multiple assembler mnemonics may appear on the same line separated by exclamation points.

A semicolon indicates that comments follow. Alternatively, you can define an entire line as a comment by beginning that line with an asterisk. You can use this feature to give individual routines in the assembly language program a *header line*, like in the following example:

```
***********************************************
***          Read Disk File Record          ***
***********************************************
```

Be sure that any labels you use are not the same as any of the assembler mnemonics, such as `MVI`, `MOV`, and `STA`. Refer to **Appendix E** for a listing of 8080 assembler mnemonics.

With the `ASM` assembler and many other assemblers, you can refer to the current value of the program counter during the assembly process. For instance, this is done automatically for program labels, as in the following example:

```
posit: EQU $
```

Arguments may be composed of various arithmetic operators. For example:

```
        MVI A,12+2*3
          /   \   |
mnemonic      arguments
```

The arithmetic operators are as follow:

`+X`	Positive number
`-X`	Negative number, corresponds to `0-X` (always 16 bit!)
`X+Y`	Addition of two 16-bit values
`X-Y`	Subtraction of two 16-bit values
`X*Y`	Product of `X*Y`
`X/Y`	Division of the arguments
`X MOD Y`	Remainder of the division `X/Y`

In addition, these two shift operators may be used:

`X SHL Y`	Shifts the 16-bit value `X` by `Y` positions to the left Bits shifted out are lost
`X SHR Y`	Shifts the 16-bit value `X` by `Y` positions to the left Bits shifted out are lost

Furthermore, these logical operators are available:

`NOT X`	Logical negation of the argument `X`
`X AND Y`	Logical `AND` of the arguments `X` and `Y`
`X OR Y`	Logical `OR` of the arguments `X` and `Y`
`X XOR Y`	Logical `XOR` of the arguments `X` and `Y`

You may not see the value of these possibilities at first glance. But you'll soon find out they are very useful. For example, if you want to load the accumulator with the high-order byte of an address label, you can easily do this by shifting this value to the right by 8 bits:

```
MVI A,label SHR 8
```

To load the lower 8 bits, you must explicitly mask the upper 8 bits. Otherwise you would load the 8-bit accumulator with a 16-bit value.

You can do this as follows:

```
MVI A,label AND 0FFH
```

In addition, there are the *pseudo-opcodes*:

```
ORG, EQU, END, DS, DB, DW, SET, IF and ENDIF
```

Pseudo-opcodes are directives to the assembler. They're called pseudo-opcodes (or simply pseudo-ops) because they are used in the assembly language program like the normal opcodes, but are not assembled and are not understood by the CPU.

We won't explain each pseudo-op in detail, but we'll mention the uses and function of each.

ORG *<start address>*

defines the starting address of the program to be assembled. `ORG` should always be the first command in a program.

EQU *<value>*

assigns a value to a label. The <value> may be an arithmetic expression.

Example: `Diskan: EQU Diskr+055H`

DS reserves a block of memory, usually for data. The program counter is incremented by the appropriate value.

Example: `Diskm: DS 100`

In this example 100 bytes are reserved. The starting address is `Diskm`, the ending address is `Diskm+99`. The following instruction starts at `Diskm+100`.

DB places the individually defined values into memory. The individual bytes are separated by commas. Strings may also be used.

Examples:

```
Disktxt:DB "Please insert the disk"
Diskt2: DB 23,32,0,3,122
```

DW places 16-bit values (words) into memory. The individual 16-bit values are separated by commas.

Example: `Diskadr: DW 03AB9H,label1`

END defines the end of the program to be assembled. For special purposes it's also possible to specify a starting address for the execution of the assembled program.

SET Similar to the `EQU` command, the `SET` command assigns a value to a label. But there is a difference: the assignment is permanent using EQU. Labels defined with `SET` may be changed during assembly. Labels defined with `SET` do not appear in the lefthand column of the assembler listing.

Examples:

```
Label1: SET Alfa
Label1: SET Label1+32
```

But we still haven't covered all the capabilities of `MAC`. Like many other capable assemblers, `ASM` can perform conditional assembly. Conditional assembly involves assembling a certain group of assembler source lines only under specific conditions. It's done with the pseudo opcodes `IF` and `ENDIF`.

Suppose that we want to write a program to read two values, and then either add them or multiply them together. The algorithm would be the same for both operations and both programs. You can write a program that checks a flag during assembly to determine if the program should add or multiply:

```
;
Multi EQU 0 ;Program is to add
ORG 0100H
;
;Read a value
CALL Read
;
IF Multi
 CALL Multir ;Call multiplication routine
ENDIF
IF NOT Multi
 Call Addir ;Call addition routine
ENDIF
CALL Output
END
```

This program is initially set to perform addition, since the value of `Multi` is set to `0`. To change the program to multiply, set the value for `Multi` equal to `NOT 0` in the first line—that's the only change that has to be made.

When you assembled the DUMP program, three files were created on diskette:

<filename>.PRN, *<filename>*.HEX, and *<filename>*.SYM

There are options to suppress these files or specify where they are written. The five options available are preceded with the $ symbol. The options are:

A	Drive for .ASM file (A-O)
H	Drive for .HEX file (A-O,Z)
L	Drive for .LIB file (A-O)
P	Drive for .PRN file (A-O, Z, P, X)
S	Drive for .SYM file (A-O, Z, P, X)

The values A through O are the drive indicators. With the '128, only A though E are possible.

The value P specifies the printer.

The value X specifies the screen.

The value Z suppresses the file.

To assemble a file DUMP.ASM on the A drive, create a printed program listing and write the hex file to the E drive, you would enter:

```
MAC DUMP $AA. PP HE
```

Notice that the options are separated by a space.

$ indicates that options follow

AA indicates that the ASM file is contained on the A drive.

PP indicates that the assembler listing is to be sent to the printer.

HE indicates that the HEX file is to be written to the E drive.

RMAC is very similar to MAC, except in can produce relocatable code in memory. When assembling, a HEX file is not created, but a REL file. The REL file is processed by the linker, LINK, unlike a HEX file which is processed by HEXCOM. Using RMAC, there are only three options for RMAC:

R	Drive for .REL file (A-O, Z)
S	Drive for .SYM file (A-O, X, P, Z)
P	Drive for .PRN file (A-O, X, P, Z)

Options are indicated by the $ symbol, and multiple options must be separated single spaces.

Next we'll discuss the disassembler/monitor SID and the use of SUBMIT files.

8.3 Working with SUBMIT

When you program in assembly language, you have to repeatedly enter a specified sequence of CP/M commands. For example, you will use the ASM to assemble the source file, convert the HEX file to a COM file and then test the new command. If the name of your program is TESTPGM, then you would have to use the following sequence of CP/M commands to assemble, convert and execute your program:

```
MAC TESTPGM
HEXCOM TESTPGM
TESTPGM
```

If you use may such sequences of commands when working with CP/M, you may want to create a SUBMIT file for each sequence. A SUBMIT file is an ordered list of CP/M commands. Later, the user can redirect the input from the keyboard to the SUBMIT file. In other words, CP/M takes the commands from the SUBMIT file rather than the keyboard.

For those of you who want to know how this takes place, here's a short explanation. When you SUBMIT a file, a temporary file called $$$.SUB. is created. It contains a copy of the original SUBMIT file, except that symbolic parameters are replaced. The CCP, which handles user input from the keyboard, recognizes the presence of and accepts the first line of input from the $$$.SUB file. (The first input line is then deleted from the $$$.SUB file).

Finally, the command contained in the first input line is executed as if it had been typed at the keyboard. When the first command line has been completely executed, the CCP returns to the $$$.SUB file to get the next input line. This is repeated until the $$$.SUB file is empty, at which time the CCP reverts back to the keyboard for subsequent input.

Let's see a practical example in action.

When you display a directory of a diskette, you'll notice that no information about the remaining space is displayed. You can get this information by using the SHOW command. Let's create a SUBMIT file, which we'll call DISP, that displays both the directory and the capacity.

To create a file called DISP.SUB we use an editor. The CP/M editor is called ED. Here's a quick lesson on the use of ED.

Insert the system diskette into the drive, making sure that the second side is face up (unless you've already made a double-sided 1571 system diskette). To create the SUBMIT file using ED, type:

```
ED DISP.SUB
```

The cursor flashes as ED waits for us to input data. ED isn't the easiest editor to use. But since we'll only be entering two lines, we won't have to suffer very long. Next, enter : to indicate that you'll be inputting characters into the file. The display will look like this:

```
: *i
1:_
```

Enter the following:

1: **show a: <RETURN>**
2: **dir <RETURN>**
3: **<CONTROL> Z**

Then exit from ED by entering the E command:

: ***E <RETURN>**

ED saves the file DISP.SUB to the diskette. You can view the file with TYPE DISP.SUB. Let's try out the new SUBMIT file. Enter:

```
SUBMIT DISP
```

Notice that the extension .SUB is not required. CP/M creates a temporary $$$.SUB file by copying the contents of DISP.SUB, and then erases the commands, line by line, from $$$.SUB as it proceeds to execute each line.

Hopefully our new SUBMIT file works: it displays the unused space on the diskette as well as the directory.

Recall our original task. We want to assemble a file, convert it into a COM file with HEXCOM, then execute it. The command sequence would like like:

```
MAC <filename> $<options>
HEXCOM <filename>
<filename>
```

Both *<filename>* and *<options>* in this example are parameters, and are separated by at least one space. A parameter may be a *specific parameter* or a *symbolic parameter.*

A specific parameter is entered as a string of characters, such as `DUMP`, `DIR` or `A:`.

A symbolic parameter is a number preceded by a dollar sign (`$`). When it is encountered in a `SUBMIT` file, a symbolic parameter is replaced by a value entered in the `SUBMIT` command line. Here's an example. This is the contents of a `SUBMIT` file called `ASSEM.COM`:

```
MAC $1 $$$2
HEXCOM $1
$1 $3
```

This is the `SUBMIT` command you enter to invoke the `SUBMIT` file above:

```
SUBMIT ASSEM DUMP AB SHOW.COM
```

The following $$$.SUB file is actually created:

```
MAC DUMP $AB
HEXCOM DUMP
DUMP SHOW.COM
```

If we return to the `SUBMIT` command line, we can see what happened. The parameters in the command line are numbered beginning with `1`.

```
SUBMIT ASSEM DUMP AB SHOW.COM
             ----  -- --------
```

parameter 1 parameter 2 parameter 3

As `SUBMIT` processes a `SUBMIT` file, it replaces the parameters in the `SUBMIT` file with the corresponding actual parameter from the command line. Thus when it encounters `$1` in the `SUBMIT` file, the first actual parameter `DUMP` is substituted. When it encounters `$$$2` in the `SUBMIT` file, the second actual parameter $AB is substituted ($$ is the notation to insert a single $). And finally, when it encounters $3, the third parameter SHOW.COM is substituted.

To reiterate about embedded $, let's give another example. Suppose you want to enter the following SUBMIT file:

```
ERA *.$$$
```

For each $, you must substitute $$. Therefore the command looks like this in a SUBMIT file:

```
ERA *.$$$$$$
```

SUBMIT is a powerful command. Besides redirecting the CCP to input commands from a SUBMIT file, you can redirect the input for other commands such as ED or PIP. These embedded commands are preceded by a less-than character (<). An example using embedded commands:

```
PIP
<E:=A:*.COM
<
DIR *.COM
```

Notice that the last input line for PIP consists of a < character. This is used to exit the transient PIP. This application could also be entered like this:

```
PIP e:=a *.COM
```

This would copy all the COM files from drive A to drive E. It's sufficient to put a < character in the first column in order to pass data to COM files. Parameters which are otherwise entered on the keyboard come from the file $$$.SUB instead.

Here we end our discussion SUBMIT files. Try making your own SUBMIT file the next time a suitable application crops up.

We've now discussed the assembler and SUBMIT files. We'll briefly mention the SID disassembler. *Disassembly* is the opposite of assembly: the machine opcodes are converted to their mnemonic equivalents. SID is not just a disassembler, but a monitor as well.

SID, an acronym for **S**ymbolic **I**nteractive **D**ebugger, allows you to test and debug programs you have developed. SID supports breakpoints, symbolic disassembly, assembly, memory display, memory fill functions, and it monitors the program execution.

To get a complete list of the SID commands listed on your printer, insert the CP/M system diskette and enter:

<CONTROL> P
HELP SID COMMANDS <RETURN>

This will list all of the SID commands to your printer. When the listing is finished enter <CONTROL> P again to turn off the printer output.

If, for example, you want to disassemble the command file HEXCOM.COM, you simply enter:

```
SID DUMP.COM
```

Before you press <RETURN>, you may press <CONTROL> P to send the output to the printer as well.

```
CP/M SID - Version 3.0
NEXT MSZE PC END
0280 0280 0100 CEFF
```

Call up the disassembler HEXCOM by entering the command L:

```
#L
0100 LXI H,0000
0103 DAD SP
.
.
.
#L180
0180 LDAZ B
0181 JNC 0189
```

The D option dumps an area of memory in hexadecimal and ASCII. The G option executes the program. The A option lets you enter source code directly with a direct assembler.

8.4 The memory layout

We have already mentioned BDOS, CCP, and BIOS. These terms are obviously very important, and you've probably heard or read them before. You may have wondered all of them are located in the computer's memory. Here's a quick overview:

CCP The Console Command Processor. This part of CP/M controls the input from the keyboard and contains the resident commands `DIR`, `ERA`, `REN`, `SAVE`, `TYPE`, and `USER`.

BDOS The Basic Disk Operating System. This part controls the transfer of data between the computer and the disk drives.

BIOS The Basic Input/Output System. The BIOS contains the machine-specific code for the CP/M operating system.The BIOS and BDOS work closely together. This is why the two are often often found under one common name: FDOS.

TPA The Transient Program Area. The TPA is the user program area in memory. The programs to be executed, and the data to be processed by these programs, are managed in this memory.

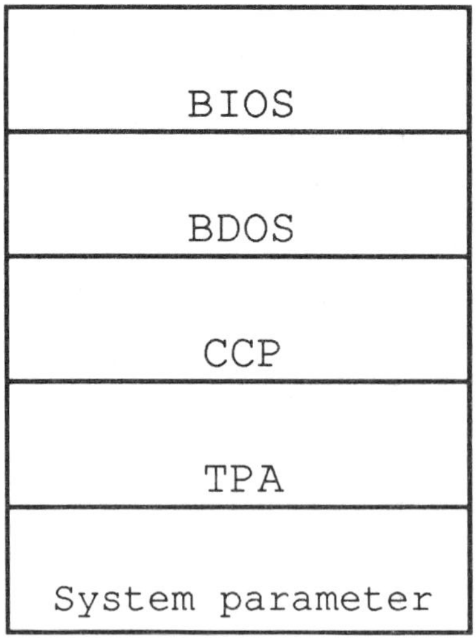

The preceding figure shows the basic memory partitions of CP/M. The user area (TPA) starts at address $0100.

The BDOS contains a collection of subroutines that performs the fundamental work with files on disk, and handles other peripheral devices. CP/M first appeared in the early 70's, which explains its obsolete routines for input and output from punch tape.

To call a BDOS routine, you must follow the standardized declarations described below:

The BDOS function code for the desired service is passed to the BDOS in the C register. Data is passed to the subroutine in the E register for 8-bit values, or the DE register pair for 16-bit values. After the registers are loaded, you jump to the BDOS at address 5 with a subroutine instruction (`CALL`).

BDOS determines the address of the desired routine from the C register. This ensures that programs written can really run on all computers, because they all follow set rules. All hardware-dependent aspects of operation, like input and output from the keyboard, are handled by special BDOS routines. When a new computer is being developed, only these routines need to be rewritten for all CP/M programs to run on the new computer.

Naturally, two preconditions must be made. The computer must have an 8080 or 8080-compatible processor, and it must be possible to read the existing programs.

If the second condition is not met, it is still theoretically possible to run CP/M programs on the new computer. Transferring existing programs has proved to be the smaller of the two problems. This can be done by

a) programming the controller, or

b) using a simple communications program to transfer the existing programs between the two computers, over a common interface such as an RS-232.

If the BDOS is to return values to the main program, 8-bit results are returned in the accumulator, while 16-bit values are returned in the HL register pair. For 16-bit return values, the accumulator contains the low-order byte, while the high-order byte is in the B register.

For example, to output a character to the console, you would use BDOS routine number 2. Let's print a question mark (using Z-80 mnemonics):

```
LD   C,2        ;CONSOLE OUTPUT
LD   E,"?"      ;LOAD QUESTION MARK
CALL 5          ;JUMP TO BDOS
```

If you want to do serious programming in machine language with CP/M, we suggest you invest in one of the many special books for CP/M programmers. They'll give you more information about the individual routines. Here we will only list the BDOS routines with input and output parameters for experimentation:

Routine name	BDOS function code	Required parameter	BDOS returns this value:
Generate warm start	0		
Console input	1		A:input
Console output	2	E:character	
Read punch tape	3		A:input
Punch tape	4	E:character	
Character to printer	5	E:character	
Direct console input	6	E:255	A:0
and output		E:character	A:character
Read IOBYTE	7		A:IOBYTE
Set IOBYTE	8	E:IOBYTE	
Output string	9	DE:=>string	
Input from buffer	10	DE:=>buffer	A:character
Console status	11		A:=0 (no key)
CP/M version	12		HL:version
Disk system reset	13		
Set reference drive	14	E:drv number	
Open file	15	DE:info	A:255 (error)
Close file	16	DE:info	A:255 (error)
Find first entry	17	DE:info	A:255 (error)
		else:	A:character
Next entry	18		A:255/character
Delete file	19	DE:info	A:255 (error)
Read sector	20	DE:info	A:0 (OK)
Write sector	21	DE:info	A:0 (OK)
Create file	22	DE:info	A:255 (error)
Rename file	23	DE:info	A:255 (error)
Read active drive	24		HL:drv vector
Read reference drive	25		A:drv number
Fix data buffer	26	DE:buffer	
Read allocation table	27		HL:address
Protect ref. drive	28		
Protected drive	29		HL:drive vector
Set file options	30	DE:info	A:255 (error)
Read disk parameters	31		HL:address
Manage user number	32	E:255	A:number
		E:number	
Read sector	33	DE:info	A:0 (OK)
Write sector	34	DE:info	A:0 (OK)
Determine file size	35	DE:info	(in buffer)
Set descriptor	36	DE:info	(in buffer)
Reset drive	37	DE:drv vector	A:0

This table is intended to show the possibilities and capabilities of the BDOS. As already mentioned, more internal knowledge of the routines is required for serious BDOS programming.

The tasks of the BIOS are even more specialized. Like the BDOS, the BIOS consists of a list of routines for data input and output. The BIOS also has routines which duplicate some of the BDOS routines, such as reading the console status.

The BIOS is largely responsible for the flexibility of CP/M, because CP/M programs can use special BIOS routines to perform hardware-dependent input and output to the console.

The BIOS is divided into four areas:

- Interface to the BDOS and CP/M programs (such as `SUBMIT` files)
- Interface to the external storage media (disk drives)
- Input and output via the peripheral addressed by the BDOS
- Buffer for data, which is stored and then made available at the appropriate time (such as with `SUBMIT` files).

The BDOS and the BIOS are relocatable in memory. The routines in the BDOS are addressed by passing the function number in the C register—and calling the fixed memory address $0005.

Calling BIOS routines is a little different than calling the BDOS.. There is a fixed jump table, but the starting address of this table can be moved. First let's take a look at the jump table:

```
00+offset JMP BOOT       ;Cold start
03+offset JMP WBOOT      ;Warm start
06+offset JMP CONST      ;Read console status
09+offset JMP CONIN      ;Console input
0C+offset JMP CONOUT     ;Console output
0F+offset JMP LIST       ;Output to printer
12+offset JMP PUNCH      ;Paper tape puncher
15+offset JMP READER     ;Paper tape reader
18+offset JMP HOME       ;Head to track 0
1B+offset JMP SELDSK     ;Select drive
1E+offset JMP SETTRK     ;Set track
21+offset JMP SETSEC     ;Select sector
24+offset JMP SETDMA     ;Select data buffer
27+offset JMP READ       ;Read sector
2A+offset JMP WRITE      ;Write sector
2D+offset JMP LISTS      ;Read printer status
30+offset JMP SECTRAN;   ;Translate sector #
```

The offset stands for the starting address in memory, which we'll soon discuss in more detail. If one of the functions is not required, such as the two routines for the punch tape, the corresponding memory addresses are filled with:

```
RET ! NOP ! NOP
```

This is used so the memory behind these routines is not moved. Jumping to this routine would cause an immediate return to the user (with no BIOS service having been performed).

To determine the BIOS starting address (the offset), we must know that address 0 of the base page of the system contains a jump to the warm start vector (the second vector in the table). This makes it easy to find the starting address. First boot up the CP/M system , then load the disassembler:

```
SID
```

To disassemble (`List`) the memory area at address 0, we enter:

```
L0000
```

SID's displays the following:

```
0000  JMP  F403
0003  RST  07
0004  NOP
0005  JMP  D300
0008  NOP            (etc.)
```

What interests us is the first line—a jump is made to address $F403. This means the BIOS jump table begins at address $F403. To jump to one of the vectors, we calculate the jump address by entering:

```
Address:=jump number * 3 + $F403
```

As with BDOS routines, you can pass parameters to the BIOS routines or receive results from them. If values are to be passed to the BIOS routines, 8-bit values are passed in the C register, while 16-bit values are passed in the BC register pair. Here you see a difference from the BDOS routines. They expect the parameter in the E register or the DE register pair. Those parameters that the BIOS routines return to the main program are returned like the BDOS routines: with 8-bit values in the accumulator. All 16-bit values are returned in the HL register pair. Since the BIOS routines are accessed via vectors in RAM, they can be changed. This allows you to write your own routines that can then return to the original program.

There a re a few additional features of the base page of the system (address $0000 to $0100). You just disassembled the area from $0000 to $0016 with the command `L0`. Several additional `JMP` instructions are found here. Especially important is the jump instruction at address 5. This is the address of the BDOS vector handler. Note that the BDOS routines for the '128 are located at $D300. The `JMP` instruction at $0005 tells us this.

Let's take a closer look at this memory area:

```
LD300
```

At $D300 is another JMP instruction, this time to $D9A4.

This concludes our introduction to the important programs and utilities in the Additional Utilities package. You should now be familiar with these additional programs. Whether they are valuable to you or not is something which you alone will decide.

Chapter 9

The Z-80 ROM listing

The Z-80 ROM listing

The '128's ROMs contain parts of the Z-80 code and are listed in the book *Commodore128 Internals*. In all, 4K of memory, an area physically located in the address range $D000 to $DFFF, are contained in the ROM.

When the Z-80 processor is activated and the Z-80 addresses memory in the range $D000 to $DFFF, the program codes located in the ROM at $D000 to $DFFF are actually addressed. The MMU (Memory Management Unit) is responsible for redirecting these addresses transparently to the user.

When the '128 is turned off and on, or a RESET is performed, the Z-80 is enabled briefly. The '128 makes the necessary preparations for a possible CP/M start; you know that the C-128 automatically boots and starts if a CP/M diskette is found in the drive on RESET. When the Z-80 is finished with its preparations the 8502 is switched back on. This then continues at exactly the place it was at when it was switched off—the place where the Z-80 was first switched on. This may sound complicated, but it's really not.

If you want to program using the Z-80, you will need to know what the Z-80 ROM contains. Furthermore, you will have to know how to program the Z-80 in the Commodore 128, because there are some characteristics which might lead to problems.

For example, if you want to address the area $D000 to $DFFF, that is, a component like the VIC, VDC, SID, etc., you can't do so with the "normal" addressing commands. The instructions `IN` and `OUT` must be used to access these "ports.". To turn on the 8502, for example, the following instructions are necessary:

```
LD  BC,$D505    ;Address Mode Configuration Register
LD  A,$B1       ;Code to turn the 8502 on
OUT (C),A       ;Corresponds to LD (BC),A
```

Correspondingly, you must use the `IN` instruction to read from memory locations. The address must always be in the BC register pair.

By carefully studying the ROM listings, you'll discover that it also contains 8502 code sequences. Enabling the processors, for example, must be given in both Z-80 and 8502 mnemonics, or it will not work. In addition, the switch must be made in a common memory area or the computer will crash after the Z-80 is turned on.

What functions does the Z-80 ROM perform?

It loads all of the necessary CP/M resident operating system routines. All screen handlers are contained in the ROMs, both for the 40-column and 80-column screens. Both the BIOS and BDOS access these ROM routines. All system messages during boot are issued by the ROM routines. Not all of the CP/M operating system is handled by the ROM; only extremely system-specific routines are found here.

Loading programs from diskette is performed by the 8502. Here the Z-80 re-enables the 8502, which then turns the Z-80 on after it has finished reading the data from diskette. In this way, the Z-80 can use the existing Kernal routines of the 8502.

Before taking a closer look at the Z-80 ROMs, there are a few things you should know. When the Z-80 is activated, several components are "rearranged."

The memory range $D000 to $DFFF is remapped to $0000. To address the logical range $D000 to $DFFF you must use `IN(X)` and `OUT(X)`.

The screen memory and character generator are also relocated. The screen memory (video RAM) is moved to $2C00. The character generator is moved to $D100. The color memory remains at {{ $Dxxx}} since it cannot be moved.

Besides the 40-column and 80-column screens there is a third screen.This third screen is used to simulate the 80-column screen. It is located at $1400 and its color RAM at $1C00. We advise you not to use this area, since it will be overwritten sooner or later.

Here is a short listing of the important addresses:

$2400	Misc temporary storage
$2402	Column for the 80-column simulation
$2404+	Mask for text output
$2406+	Address cursor 40-column screen
$2408	Lines per screen (default 24)
$2409+	Cursor address + $1400 for 80-column simulation
$240B	Cursor column (40 column)
$240C	Cursor line (40 column)
$240D	Character color
$240E	Background color
$240F	Border color
$2410	Fill char (either $00 or $80) for reverse space
$2411	Cursor address
$2413	Cursor column
$2414	Cursor line
$2415	Attribute
$2416	Background color 80 column screen
$2417	Foreground color 80 column screen
$FD01	Flag for set vectors yes/no
$FD03	Track to read
$FD04	Sector to read
$FD05	Number of blocks to be loaded yet
$FD06	Error flag ($00, $0D, $FF)
$FD08	Logical filenumber
$FD0D	Pointer to conversion table
$FD10	Attack/decay
$FD11	Volume
$FD12	Frequency (hi)
$FD13	Sustain/release
$FD14	Turn sound off
$FD15	Turn sound on
$FD18	Base address of block to load

\+ The addresses marked with "+" are to be interpreted as 16-bit values.

The CP/M boot sector is identified as such by the three letters CBM followed by five bytes containing zero. The program looks like this:

```
SEI          Disable interrupts
JSR $FF84    IOINIT
LDA #$3E     Define
STA $FF00    Configuration byte
LDA #$C3     Code for JP under Z-80
STA $FFEE    Store code
LDA #$08     Low byte is $08
STA $FFEF    Store
LDA #$00     High byte is $00
STA $FFF0    Store; corresponds to RST $08
JMP $FFD0    Turn Z-80 on
```

This is all that the boot sector does. Everything else is performed by the Z-80 ROM.

Memory areas which are copied are specified with two addresses. First the physical/logical address and then the destination address. Relative jumps refer to their intended memory environment.

Now to the ROM listing:

```
********************************* RST 00 (cold start)

0000:  3E 3E      LD    A,$3E       configuration byte
                                    (RAM,I/O)
0002:  32 00 FF   LD    ($FF00),A   into config. register
0005:  C3 3B 00   JP    $003B       cold start rest


********************************* RST 08; turn Z-80 on again

0008:  31 77 3C   LD    SP,$3C77    SP initialization
000B:  3E 3F      LD    A,$3F       configuration byte
000D:  C3 8C 01   JP    $018C       RST-08-Routine's rest

********************************* RST 10

0010:  E1         POP   HL          Stack's return address
0011:  6E         LD    L,(HL)      retrieve following byte
                                     as offset
0012:  C3 20 00   JP    $0020       Start RST-20-Routine
0015:  00         NOP               Fill bytes
0016:  00         NOP
0017:  00         NOP


********************************* RST 18

0018:  E1         POP   HL          Stack's return address
0019:  6E         LD    L,(HL)      Lo-Byte of  return address
001A:  C3 28 00   JP    $0028       start RST-28-Routine
001D:  00         NOP               Fill bytes
001E:  00         NOP
001F:  00         NOP


********************************* RST 20

0020:  3A 0F FD   LD    A,($FD0F)
0023:  A7         AND   A           Set Flags
0024:  28 02      JR    Z,$0028     Return on nullflag
0026:  2C         INC   L           otherwise increment the
0027:  2C         INC   L           return pointer to 2
```

```
********************************* RST 28; retrieve
                                  return address
                                  from table

0028:  26 01     LD    H,$01     Hi-Byte of table is 1
002A:  7E        LD    A,(HL)    offset
002B:  23        INC   HL        pointer now to Hi-Byte
002C:  66        LD    H,(HL)    retrieve also Hi-Byte
002D:  6F        LD    L,A       Lo-Byte to  L
002E:  E9        JP    (HL)      And return indirectly
002F:  00        NOP             Fill byte


********************************* RST 30; Dummy;
                                  construction data

0030:  30 35 2F 31 32 2F 38 35    .ASC "05/12/85"
                                  =June 12, 1985


********************************* RST 38

0038:  C3 FD FD  JP    $FDFD     Continue RST 38 on $FDFD


************************************ RST 0 Contn'd

003B:  01 2F D0  LD    BC,$D02F  Register 47 of VICchip
                                 (Keyboard)
003E:  11 FC FF  LD    DE,$FFFC  write $FF to the keyboard
0041:  ED 51     OUT   (C),D     no extension keys
0043:  03        INC   BC        Register 48=clock register
0044:  ED 59     OUT   (C),E     set $FC to -> 1 MHz-Mode
0046:  01 05 D5  LD    BC,$D505  Mode configurtion Register
0049:  3E B0     LD    A,$B0     /EXROM and /GAME test,
004B:  ED 79     OUT   (C),A     and turn on 128-Mode
004D:  ED 78     IN    A,(C)     Mode configurtion Register
004F:  2F        CPL             read out again and negate
0050:  E6 30     AND   $30       /EXROM oder  GAME set?
0052:  28 05     JR    Z,$0059   No, then no carriage ret
```

```
*******************************       turn on 64-Mode and
                                      turn control
                                      over to cartridge

0054:  3E F1     LD    A,$F1          turn on 8502 and select
0056:  ED 79     OUT   (C),A          the 64-mode
0058:  C7        RST   $00            and carry out cold start
0059:  01 0F DC  LD    BC,$DC0F       CRB-Register in CIA 1
005C:  3E 08     LD    A,$08          select and then
005E:  ED 79     OUT   (C),A          stop Timer B and
0060:  0D        DEC   C              Timer A of
0061:  ED 79     OUT   (C),A          CIA 1
0063:  0E 03     LD    C,$03          DDRB-data direction
                                       register
0065:  AF        XOR   A              for Port B:set all bits
0066:  ED 79     OUT   (C),A          forinput
0068:  0D        DEC   C              set pointer to DDRA and
0069:  3D        DEC   A              all bits here to
006A:  ED 79     OUT   (C),A          output
006C:  0D        DEC   C              After decrementing 3 times
006D:  0D        DEC   C              show BC on Port A
006E:  3E 7F     LD    A,$7F          Port A with $7F (See also
0070:  ED 79     OUT   (C),A          keyboard matrix) describe
0072:  03        INC   BC             pointer to Port B (input)
0073:  ED 78     IN    A,(C)          and read out
0075:  E6 20     AND   $20            Commodore-key masking
0077:  01 05 D5  LD    BC,$D505       pointer for
                                       Mode-config.-Reg.
007A:  28 D8     JR    Z,$0054        was hit-> 64er-Mode
007C:  21 B4 0F  LD    HL,$0FB4       Now set the  Register of
007F:  01 0A D5  LD    BC,$D50A       the MMU with the values
0082:  16 0B     LD    D,$0B          from $0FAA
0084:  7E        LD    A,(HL)         Note, that all
0085:  ED 79     OUT   (C),A          11 Registers of MMU
0087:  2B        DEC   HL             from behind with values
0088:  0D        DEC   C              will be described
                                       from $0FB4
0089:  15        DEC   D              downward!
008A:  20 F8     JR    NZ,$0084       Loop end
008C:  21 1A 0D  LD    HL,$0D1A       Copy the area from $0D1A
008F:  11 00 11  LD    DE,$1100       to $1100
0092:  01 08 00  LD    BC,$0008       Eight Bytes are to be
0095:  ED B0     LDIR                 copied (8502-Code!)
```

```
0097:  21 E5 0E   LD    HL,$0EE5  Also copy the area
009A:  11 D0 FF   LD    DE,$FFD0  from $0EE5 on until Common
009D:  01 1F 00   LD    BC,$001F  Area from $FFD0
00A0:  ED B0      LDIR            31 Bytes are to be copied
00A2:  21 00 11   LD    HL,$1100  $1100 as return vector
00A5:  22 FA FF   LD    ($FFFA),HL copy return vector in
00A8:  22 FC FF   LD    ($FFFC),HL all 4 addresses,
00AB:  22 FE FF   LD    ($FFFE),HL under other
00AE:  22 DD FF   LD    ($FFDD),HL also on $FFDD
                                   (freshly copied)
00B1:  C3 E0 FF   JP    $FFE0     and return in Z-80-part


*********************************

00B4:  CD 6D 03   CALL  $036D     Load Block
00B7:  3A 06 3C   LD    A,($3C06) get block number
00BA:  22 18 FD   LD    ($FD18),H Destination address of
                                   loaded block
00BD:  11 ED 00   LD    DE,$00E D
00C0:  F5         PUSH  AF        Save block number
00C1:  CD D3 00   CALL  $00D3     compare  (HL) with (DE)
00C4:  CC FA 02   CALL  Z,$02FA   If ok, then call
00C7:  F1         POP   AF        get block number back
00C8:  2A 18 FD   LD    HL,($FD18 Get load address
00CB:  11 20 00   LD    DE,$0020  32 as Offset
00CE:  19         ADD   HL,DE     add to each other
00CF:  3D         DEC   A         Decrement block counter
00D0:  20 E8      JR    NZ,$00BA  still not done, then loop
00D2:  C9         RET             End of the subroutine


********************************* compare (HL) with (DE)

00D3:  06 0C      LD    B,$0C     12 Bytes to be compared
00D5:  EB         EX    DE,HL     Exchange the two
                                  compared registers
00D6:  1A         LD    A,(DE)    Load the first value
                                  in accumulator
00D7:  E6 7F      AND   $7F       and erase the  8th Bit
00D9:  BE         CP    (HL)      compare with (HL) lead
                                  through
00DA:  C0         RET   NZ        and break off if different
```

```
00DB:  23         INC   HL         otherwise increment
                                   both addresses
00DC:  13         INC   DE         by one
00DD:  10 F7      DJNZ  $00D6      and loop
00DF:  3A 06 3C   LD    A,($3C06)  Get block number
00E2:  FE 40      CP    $40        64 Blocks zu load?
00E4:  1A         LD    A,(DE)     Get block # from table
00E5:  20 01      JR    NZ,$00E8   $3C06 is smaller than 64
00E7:  1F         RRA              otherwise double accu
00E8:  32 35 3C   LD    ($3C35),   and note
00EB:  AF         XOR   A          Erase accu and Flags
00EC:  C9         RET              Routine's end


********************************** Text

00ED:  00         NOP
00EE:  43 50 4D 2B 20 20 20 20    "CPM+"
00F6:  53 59 53 00                "SYS" <End>


********************************** Compare HL with DE

00FA:  7C         LD    A,H        Hi-Byte of  HL
00FB:  BA         CP    D          compare with D
00FC:  C0         RET   NZ         and end, when different
00FD:  7D         LD    A,L        otherwise compare
00FE:  BB         CP    E          the Lo-Bytes from
                                   HL and DE
00FF:  C9         RET              and return with Flags


********************************** return table for RST 28

0100:  84 06          .Word $0684  64 Return addresses
0102:  6E 09          .Word $096E

0104:  AB 06          .Word $06AB
0106:  BC 09          .Word $09BC
0108:  C2 06          .Word $06C2
010A:  DD 09          .Word $09DD
010C:  D1 06          .Word $06D1
010E:  F1 09          .Word $09F1
```

```
0110:  DD 06        .Word $06DD
0112:  31 0A        .Word $0A31
0114:  E8 06        .Word $06E8

0116:  3C 0A        .Word $0A3C

0118:  F1 06        .Word $06F1
011A:  45 0A        .Word $0A45

011C:  7A 07        .Word $077A
011E:  48 0A        .Word $0A48
0120:  80 07        .Word $0780
0122:  62 0A        .Word $0A62
0124:  91 07        .Word $0791
0126:  8E 0A        .Word $0A8E
0128:  CA 07        .Word $07CA
012A:  BA 0A        .Word $0ABA
012C:  DC 07        .Word $07DC
012E:  DF 0A        .Word $0ADF
0130:  1E 08        .Word $081E
0132:  2D 0B        .Word $0B2D
0134:  1B 07        .Word $071B
0136:  7B 0B        .Word $0B7B
0138:  10 07        .Word $0710
013A:  62 0B        .Word $0B62
013C:  1C 09        .Word $091C
013E:  95 09        .Word $0995
0140:  27 09        .Word $0927
0142:  A2 09        .Word $09A2
0144:  4E 07        .Word $074E
0146:  AE 0B        .Word $0BAE
0148:  EB 00        .Word $00EB
014A:  EB 00        .Word $00EB
014C:  EB 00        .Word $00EB
014E:  EB 00        .Word $00EB
0150:  E3 03        .Word $03E3
0152:  6B 04        .Word $046B
0154:  FA 0C        .Word $0CFA
0156:  EB 00        .Word $00EB
0158:  EB 00        .Word $00EB
015A:  EB 00        .Word $00EB
015C:  EB 00        .Word $00EB
015E:  EB 00        .Word $00EB
```

```
0160:  3C 0C          .Word $0C3C
0162:  4A 0C          .Word $0C4A
0164:  CF 0B          .Word $0BCF
0166:  0C 0C          .Word $0C0C
0168:  26 05          .Word $0526
016A:  32 05          .Word $0532
016C:  2C 05          .Word $052C
016E:  EB 00          .Word $00EB
0170:  7F 0C          .Word $0C7F
0172:  C2 0C          .Word $0CC2
0174:  C7 0C          .Word $0CC7
0176:  E4 0C          .Word $0CE4
0178:  EB 00          .Word $00EB
017A:  3D 08          .Word $083D
017C:  AE 08          .Word $08AE
017E:  60 06          .Word $0660
0780:  C3 0A          .Word $0AC3
0182:  09          ADD   HL,BC         Add BC as Offset
0183:  C3 33 09    JP    $0933         Get A:attribute, B:char on
                                       (HL) in VDC


********************************** HL as Update address in
                                   VDC

0186:  C3 53 09    JP    $0953         HL as Update address
                                       in VDC


********************************** wait for VDC-Status and
                                   choose register <accu>

0189:  C3 45 09    JP    $0945         wait for VDC-Status and
                                       choose <accu>


********************************** RST 8 Contn'd

018C:  32 00 FF    LD    ($FF00),A     accu into config. byte
018F:  21 00 30    LD    HL,$3000      The areas
0192:  11 01 30    LD    DE,$3001      $3000 to  $FEFF
0195:  01 FF CE    LD    BC,$CEFF      will be filled with
0198:  75          LD    (HL),L        the value $00
```

```
0199:  ED B0     LDIR
019B:  21 22 0D  LD    HL,$0D22   The area from $0D22
019E:  11 00 30  LD    DE,$3000   will be copied to $3000
01A1:  01 C3 01  LD    BC,$01C3   Here it works with
01A4:  ED B0     LDIR             8502-Code!
01A6:  21 E5 0E  LD    HL,$0EE5   Area down
01A9:  11 D0 FF  LD    DE,$FFD0   $0EE5 in Common Area
01AC:  01 1F 00  LD    BC,$001F   Copy from $FFD0
01AF:  ED B0     LDIR             31 Bytes
01B1:  3E C9     LD    A,$C9      Code for RETurn
01B3:  32 EE FF  LD    ($FFEE),A  Set RST 8 with RET
01B6:  CD E0 FF  CALL  $FFE0      Turn on 8502,then continue
01B9:  21 B4 0F  LD    HL,$0FB4   The MMU-Register
01BC:  01 0A D5  LD    BC,$D50A   will be filled with the
                                  table
01BF:  16 0B     LD    D,$0B      from $0FAA
01C1:  7E        LD    A,(HL)     s.o.
01C2:  ED 79     OUT   (C),A      s.o.
01C4:  2B        DEC   HL         s.o.
01C5:  0D        DEC   C          s.o.
01C6:  15        DEC   D          s.o.
01C7:  20 F8     JR    NZ,$01C1   End of the loop
01C9:  21 00 10  LD    HL,$1000   Fill the area
01CC:  11 01 10  LD    DE,$1001   $1000 to  $2FFF
01CF:  01 FF 1F  LD    BC,$1FFF   with the value
01D2:  75        LD    (HL),L     $00
01D3:  ED B0     LDIR             s.o.
01D5:  3E 1A     LD    A,$1A      Register 26 (color) of VDC
01D7:  CD 45 09  CALL  $0945      choose and then front/
01DA:  3E 90     LD    A,$90      Set Background color
01DC:  ED 79     OUT   (C),A      on VDC to $90
                                  (light red Cursor)
01DE:  3E 83     LD    A,$83      Define light blue
                                   and alternate
01E0:  32 15 24  LD    ($2415),A  har set as attributes
                                  (VDC)
01E3:  3E 0E     LD    A,$0E      Define Char color for
                                  VIC-Chip
01E5:  32 0D 24  LD    ($240D),A
01E8:  CD BD 05  CALL  $05BD      Prepare VDC-char set
01EB:  3E 19     LD    A,$19      The screen is defined
                                  with  24
01ED:  32 08 24  LD    ($2408),A  lines (DEVICE)
```

```
01F0:  CD 26 05    CALL  $0526      Output the following text
01F3:  FF          .Byte $FF        erase screen ($FF)
01F4:  81 0A       .Byte $81,$0A    line 1, column 10
01F5:  42 4F 4F 54 49 4E 47 20      BOOTING
01FD:  43 50 2F 4D 20 50 4C 55      CP/M PLUS
0205:  53 00                        US<End>
0208:  01 18 D0    LD    BC,$D018   Basis address of Video-RAM
020B:  3E B6       LD    A,$B6      B->10-13 Video-RAM,
                                    6->11-13
020D:  ED 79       OUT   (C),A      CHARROM; Videoram from
                                    $2C00
020F:  CD D2 02    CALL  $02D2      Boot sector check and
                                    retrieve
0212:  C2 FF 04    JP    NZ,$04FF   Output evtl. errors
0215:  21 B2 0F    LD    HL,$0FB2   Mark table beginning
0218:  22 02 3C    LD    ($3C02),H  in $3C02
021B:  CD B4 00    CALL  $00B4      Load first part
021E:  CD B4 00    CALL  $00B4      Load second part
0221:  2A 09 3C    LD    HL,($3C09  Retrieve value
0224:  7C          LD    A,H        Set the zero flag
0225:  B5          OR    L          if the 16-bit value is 0
0226:  CA FF 04    JP    Z,$04FF    and return if yes
0229:  21 09 3C    LD    HL,$3C09   Mark new table beginning
022C:  22 02 3C    LD    ($3C02),HL
022F:  CD 6D 03    CALL  $036D      Load dat
0232:  21 00 34    LD    HL,$3400   Copy 12 Bytes
0235:  11 29 3C    LD    DE,$3C29   from $3400
0238:  01 0C 00    LD    BC,$000C   to $3C29
023B:  ED B0       LDIR
023D:  CD 26 05    CALL  $0526      Output blank line
0240:  8A          .Byte $8A,$00,$00 line 10, column 0 and
                                    <End>
0243:  21 80 34    LD    HL,$3480   pointer to output text
0246:  CD 34 05    CALL  $0534      and output Text from (HL)
0249:  21 00 35    LD    HL,$3500   Note pointer $3500
024C:  22 04 3C    LD    ($3C04),HL
024F:  CD 26 05    CALL  $0526      Ouput the following text
0252:  83          .Byte $83,$0C    line 3, column 12
0254:  44 41 54 41 20 54 41 42      DATA TAB
025C:  4C 45 53 00                  LES<End>
0260:  2A 33 3C    LD    HL,($3C33) Load CP/M segments
0263:  22 09 FD    LD    ($FD09),HL one after the other into
0266:  21 32 3C    LD    HL,$3C32   work memory
```

```
0269:  CD 31 03   CALL  $0331      Get block number and
                                   Start address
026C:  22 0B FD   LD    ($FD0B),H  Note Start address
026F:  CD 44 03   CALL  $0344
0272:  11 80 00   LD    DE,$0080   Add Record offset
                                   (CP/M-Intern)
0275:  19         ADD   HL,DE      from 128
0276:  20 F7      JR    NZ,$026F   If still not finished,
                                   then output
0278:  CD 26 05   CALL  $0526      the following text
027B:  84 0C      .Byte $84,$0C    line 4, column 12
027D:  43 4F 4D 4D 4F 4E 20 43     COMMON C
0285:  4F 44 45 00                 ODE<End>
0289:  21 2A 3C   LD    HL,$3C2A   Basis address for Table
028C:  CD 24 03   CALL  $0324      and load Common Code
028F:  CD 26 05   CALL  $0526      output the following text
0292:  85 0C      .Byte $85,$0C    line 5, column 12
0294:  42 41 4E 4B 45 44 20 43     BANKED C
029C:  4F 44 45 00                 ODE<End>
02A0:  21 2C 3C   LD    HL,$3C2C   Basis address for Table
02A3:  CD 24 03   CALL  $0324      and load Banked Code
02A6:  CD 26 05   CALL  $0526      Output the following text
02A9:  86 0C      .Byte $86,$0C    line 6, column 12
02AB:  42 49 4F 53 38 35 30 32     BIOS8502
02B3:  20 43 4F 44 45 00           CODE<Ende>
02B9:  21 30 3C   LD    HL,$3C30   Basis address for Table
02BC:  CD 24 03   CALL  $0324      and load BIOS8502 Data
02BF:  3A 30 3C   LD    A,($3C30)
02C2:  47         LD    B,A
02C3:  3A 2F 3C   LD    A,($3C2F)
02C6:  90         SUB   B          Form a difference
02C7:  32 DE FF   LD    ($FFDE),A Difference as Hi-Byte
02CA:  AF         XOR   A          accu erase (=0)
02CB:  32 DD FF   LD    ($FFDD),A Mark as Lo-Byte
02CE:  2A 2D 3C   LD    HL,($3C2D) return address for
                                   CP/M-return
02D1:  E9         JP    (HL)       retrieve and return
```

```
********************************** Read from track 1/Sector 0

02D2:   21 00 FE   LD     HL,$FE00  Note  load address for
                                    first to load
02D5:   22 18 FD   LD     ($FD18),H Block
02D8:   AF         XOR    A         accu erase
02D9:   32 04 FD   LD     ($FD04),A Sector#=0
02DC:   3C         INC    A         accu=1
02DD:   32 03 FD   LD     ($FD03),A Define track
02E0:   CD 4F 04   CALL   $044F     Read track/Sector
02E3:   CD 6B 04   CALL   $046B     If read, test boot sector
02E6:   C0         RET    NZ        No  Boot sector
02E7:   3C         INC    A         Last character of the
                                    block+1
02E8:   21 00 38   LD     HL,$3800  Start address
02EB:   3E 20      LD     A,$20     32 as Block counter
02ED:   20 03      JR     NZ,$02F2  If accu before
                                    INC<>$FF, return
02EF:   26 3C      LD     H,$3C     change Hi-Byte to  $3C
02F1:   87         ADD    A,A       and double block number
                                    (Record number)
02F2:   22 07 3C   LD     ($3C07),H Note load address
02F5:   32 06 3C   LD     ($3C06),  Note block number
02F8:   AF         XOR    A         erase accu and
                                    Flags (important)
02F9:   C9         RET              and End the Routine


**********************************

02FA:   11 09 3C   LD     DE,$3C09  Load address for copy
02FD:   3A 35 3C   LD     A,($3C35) Get Flag
0300:   B7         OR     A         Set Flags
0301:   28 07      JR     Z,$030A   Flag isn't set
0303:   11 19 3C   LD     DE,$3C19  otherwise Start address+16
0306:   3D         DEC    A         and decrement flag
                                    (counter)
0307:   C2 80 04   JP     NZ,$0480  and output errors
030A:   2A 18 FD   LD     HL,($FD18) Get goal address
030D:   01 10 00   LD     BC,$0010  16 as Increment
0310:   09         ADD    HL,BC     add
0311:   ED B0      LDIR             and copy 16 Bytes
```

```
0313:  3A 09 3C    LD    A,($3C09) Get counter and
0316:  B7          OR    A         set Flags
0317:  C8          RET   Z         On zero, the work is done
0318:  2A 18 3C    LD    HL,($3C18 Else get address
031B:  AF          XOR   A         and compare with $0000
031C:  BD          CP    L         accu is zero
031D:  28 02       JR    Z,$0321   Lo-Byte is zero
031F:  BC          CP    H         compare with Hi-Byte
0320:  C8          RET   Z         Hi-Byte is zero
0321:  C3 29 02    JP    $0229     Zero flag will be
                                  passed as Parameter


********************************* Load  Records from Floppy

0324:  CD 31 03    CALL  $0331     Get number & start address
0327:  11 80 FF    LD    DE,$FF80  128 as two's complement
032A:  19          ADD   HL,DE     add (flag!)
032B:  CD 44 03    CALL  $0344     Load record
032E:  20 F7       JR    NZ,$0327  Another  Record
0330:  C9          RET             otherwise end of  Routine


********************************* Get number Start address

0331:  5E          LD    E,(HL)    Get number
0332:  16 00       LD    D,$00     and erase Hi-Byte
0334:  7B          LD    A,E       Test number
0335:  B7          OR    A         against zero
0336:  CA 1B 05    JP    Z,$051B   BAD if zero
0339:  EB          EX    DE,HL     otherwise number to HL
033A:  29          ADD   HL,HL     and double (Record number)
033B:  22 00 3C    LD    ($3C00),HL note in $3C00
033E:  EB          EX    DE,HL     again to  DE
033F:  2B          DEC   HL        Decrement table pointer
0340:  66          LD    H,(HL)    Get Hi-Byte
0341:  2E 00       LD    L,$00     and erase Lo-Byte
0343:  C9          RET             End of the Routine
```

```
********************************* Load Record and
                                  decrement counter

0344:  E5          PUSH  HL          Save to stack
0345:  2A 07 3C    LD    HL,($3C07)  Save the comparison
                                     address
0348:  EB          EX    DE,HL       and mark in DE
0349:  2A 04 3C    LD    HL,($3C04)  Get second comparison
                                     address
034C:  CD FA 00    CALL  $00FA       Compare (HL) with  (DE)
034F:  CC 6D 03    CALL  Z,$036D     and  return, if the same
0352:  EB          EX    DE,HL       else exchange the
                                     register again
0353:  21 80 00    LD    HL,$0080    Record-Offset of  128
0356:  19          ADD   HL,DE       add to each other
0357:  22 04 3C    LD    ($3C04),HL  and note again
035A:  E1          POP   HL          call address back again
035B:  E5          PUSH  HL          & restore safely to stack
035C:  EB          EX    DE,HL       Exchange goal and source
035D:  01 80 00    LD    BC,$0080    and copy 128 Bytes
0360:  ED B0       LDIR              (1 Record)
0362:  2A 00 3C    LD    HL,($3C00)  Get  Record counter
0365:  2B          DEC   HL          Decrement by one
0366:  22 00 3C    LD    ($3C00),HL  and store again
0369:  7D          LD    A,L         Test if record number
036A:  B4          OR    H           is exactly zero, set flags
036B:  E1          POP   HL          call address back
036C:  C9          RET               and end Routine


********************************* Load data from
                                  $3400 + Offset

036D:  21 00 34    LD    HL,$3400    Load address (Basis)
0370:  22 18 FD    LD    ($FD18),H   Note for 8502-Code
0373:  E5          PUSH  HL          and push to  Stack
0374:  2A 02 3C    LD    HL,($3C02)  pointer to  Block load
                                     table
0377:  16 00       LD    D,$00       Erase Hi-Byte
0379:  5E          LD    E,(HL)      and get Lo-Byte from Table
037A:  23          INC   HL          Increment pointer to Table
037B:  22 02 3C    LD    ($3C02),HL  and note again
037E:  EB          EX    DE,HL       Number blocks to HL
```

```
037F:  29         ADD   HL,HL       and double ->,Record no.
0380:  29         ADD   HL,HL       double again
0381:  3A 06 3C   LD    A,($3C06)   Get block number
0384:  0F         RRCA              /2
0385:  0F         RRCA              /4
0386:  0F         RRCA              /8
0387:  FE 04      CP    $04         Is block number 32 - 63??
0389:  28 01      JR    Z,$038C     Yes, then return
038B:  29         ADD   HL,HL       else double HL again
038C:  22 16 FD   LD    ($FD16),HL  Note us as Block number
                                     (load CP/M)
038F:  3D         DEC   A           Decrement number to
                                     loaded Blocks
0390:  32 05 FD   LD    ($FD05),A   and otherwise note
0393:  F5         PUSH  AF          Save number to Stack
0394:  3E 01      LD    A,$01       Number to the
                                     loaded data blocks
0396:  32 BD 31   LD    ($31BD),A   set to 1
0399:  CD E3 03   CALL  $03E3       Set to Block# ->
                                    Track/Sector
039C:  2A 16 FD   LD    HL,($FD16)Get  Block number
039F:  23         INC   HL          Increment by one and
03A0:  22 16 FD   LD    ($FD16),HL lay down again
03A3:  F1         POP   AF          Get counter and Flags
03A4:  28 2A      JR    Z,$03D0     If end, then return
03A6:  3A 08 FD   LD    A,($FD08)   Else get error flag
03A9:  A7         AND   A           and set Flags
03AA:  28 24      JR    Z,$03D0     No errors
03AC:  2A 03 FD   LD    HL,($FD03)  Get Track/Sector
03AF:  E5         PUSH  HL          and save to stack
03B0:  CD E3 03   CALL  $03E3       wander Block# in
                                    Track/Sector
03B3:  E1         POP   HL          calculate Track/Sector,
                                     call back
03B4:  3A 03 FD   LD    A,($FD03)   Get track#
03B7:  BD         CP    L           Compare with calculated
                                    track
03B8:  20 13      JR    NZ,$03CD    they are different
03BA:  E5         PUSH  HL          save Track/Sector
03BB:  2A 16 FD   LD    HL,($FD16   Get Block#
03BE:  23         INC   HL          and increment Block number
03BF:  22 16 FD   LD    ($FD16),HL Note new Block number
```

```
03C2:  21 BD 31   LD    HL,$31BD  pointer to loaded Block
                                  number
03C5:  34         INC   (HL)      and also increment
03C6:  21 05 FD   LD    HL,$FD05  Still to loaded Block
                                  number
03C9:  35         DEC   (HL)      also increment by 1
                                  (error correction)
03CA:  20 E4      JR    NZ,$03B0  still at least one  Block
03CC:  E1         POP   HL        Get Track/Sektor from
                                  Stack
03CD:  22 03 FD   LD    ($FD03),HL Note  Track/Sektor


********************************* Error walk

03D0:  CD 4F 04   CALL  $044F     Read Block/Blocks
                                  from Diskette
03D3:  21 19 FD   LD    HL,$FD19  Hi-Byte destination
                                  address

03D6:  3A BD 31   LD    A,($31BD) Get number to loaded block
03D9:  86         ADD   A,(HL)    Add to destination address
03DA:  77         LD    (HL),A    and note
03DB:  3A 05 FD   LD    A,($FD05) Get number to loaded
                                  blocks
03DE:  A7         AND   A         Set flags
03DF:  20 AE      JR    NZ,$038F  Continue, if not yet
                                  finished
03E1:  E1         POP   HL        else get Track/Sektor
03E2:  C9         RET             and End the Routine


*****************************     Make out of Block#
                                  Track/Sector

03E3:  3E 23      LD    A,$23     35 as Offset for 1571
                                  (Side 2)
03E5:  32 00 24   LD    ($2400),A and mark Offset
03E8:  2A 16 FD   LD    HL,($FD16)Get  Block#
03EB:  11 A8 02   LD    DE,$02A8  from Block # $2A8 ->
                                  address side 2
03EE:  B7         OR    A         Carry for subtraction
                                  erase
```

```
03EF:  ED 52      SBC   HL,DE      absolute Blocknumber on
                                   side 2
03F1:  30 05      JR    NC,$03F8   Find out by subtraction
                                   return on side 1
03F3:  AF         XOR   A          Offset erase
03F4:  32 00 24   LD    ($2400),A  and save
03F7:  19         ADD   HL,DE      subtraction correction
03F8:  23         INC   HL         Block# + 2, there 1./2.
                                   Block
03F9:  23         INC   HL         Reserved for Directory
03FA:  11 65 01   LD    DE,$0165   (357) Block number from
                                   track 19
03FD:  01 00 15   LD    BC,$1500   track 0- has 21
                                   sectors/track
0400:  B7         OR    A          erase carry for
                                   subtraction
0401:  ED 52      SBC   HL,DE      Control on 21
                                   sectors/track
0403:  38 1B      JR    C,$0420    Yes, Block lies in
                                   21-sectors-area
0405:  23         INC   HL         +1 for error correction
0406:  11 85 00   LD    DE,$0085   Have the next 133 blocks
0409:  01 11 13   LD    BC,$1311   17 sectors per track
040C:  ED 52      SBC   HL,DE      Test if block is in this
                                   area
040E:  38 10      JR    C,$0420    Yes, then end series of
                                   tests
0410:  11 6C 00   LD    DE,$006C   Have next track
0413:  01 18 12   LD    BC,$1218   18 sectors/track  (from
                                   track  $18)
0416:  ED 52      SB    HL,DE      Test if block is in this
                                   area
0418:  38 06      JR    C,$0420    Yes, then end test series
041A:  11 00 00   LD    DE,$0000   correction factor to zero
041D:  01 1E 11   LD    BC,$111E   from track  30-17 sectors
0420:  19         ADD   HL,DE      Subtraction correction
0421:  16 00      LD    D,$00      Erase Hi-Byte from DE
0423:  58         LD    E,B        sector to E
0424:  B7         OR    A          Erase Carry
0425:  0C         INC   C          Increment track
0426:  ED 52      SBC   HL,DE      subtract sectors per track
0428:  30 FB      JR    NC,$0425   and evtl. continue looping
042A:  19         ADD   HL,DE      error correction
```

```
042B:  3A 00 24   LD    A,($2400) Get Offset for page 0/1
042E:  81         ADD   A,C       add Offset to track
042F:  32 03 FD   LD    ($FD03),A Note calculated track
0432:  E5         PUSH  HL        Save  sector# to Stack
0433:  21 B5 0F   LD    HL,$0FB5  Table for adjusted sector
                                  numbers
0436:  01 15 00   LD    BC,$0015  To optimize access
0439:  7B         LD    A,E       Get sector number and
043A:  B9         CP    C         compare with maximal value
043B:  28 0A      JR    Z,$0447   Is 21, then end
043D:  09         ADD   HL,BC     else add Offset for table
                                  pointer
043E:  0B         DEC   BC        Next area has 2 sectors
043F:  0B         DEC   BC        fewer per  track
0440:  B9         CP    C         Has the maximal value been
                                  reached?
0441:  28 04      JR    Z,$0447   Yes, then end
0443:  09         ADD   HL,BC     else add Offset for next
                                  area
0444:  0B         DEC   BC        Next area has one sector
0445:  18 F9      JR    $0440     fewer and cont. searching
0447:  C1         POP   BC        Get sector# from Stack
0448:  09         ADD   HL,BC     and add to Basis
0449:  7E         LD    A,(HL)    Get adjusted  sector #
044A:  32 04 FD   LD    ($FD04),  and note
044D:  3C         INC   A         Erase flags and
044E:  C9         RET             End block calculations
```

```
********************************* Reading from disk

044F:  3E 03     LD    A,$03       Set number of read tries
0451:  32 36 3C  LD    ($3C36),A   on the floppy
0454:  3E 01     LD    A,$01       set the flag for vector
0456:  32 01 FD  LD    ($FD01),A   (won't be set again)
0459:  CD 8C 05  CALL  $058C       Show Block (Track/sector)
                                   on the screen
045C:  CD E0 FF  CALL  $FFE0       Turn on 8502
045F:  3E 3F     LD    A,$3F       Turn on Configuration byte
                                   RAM Bank 0
0461:  32 00 FF  LD    ($FF00),A
0464:  3A 06 FD  LD    A,($FD06    Get read error flag
0467:  B7        OR    A           and test for read errors
0468:  20 32     JR    NZ,$049C    Read read errors
046A:  C9        RET               Else end the routine


********************************  Test loaded block on
                                  boot sector

046B:  21 00 FE  LD    HL,$FE00   Start address of
                                  loaded  Block
046E:  7E        LD    A,(HL)     Get first character
046F:  FE 43     CP    $43        is it  "C"?
0471:  C0        RET   NZ         No, then not a boot sector
0472:  2C        INC   L          get next  character
0473:  7E        LD    A,(HL)     and
0474:  FE 42     CP    $42        compare with "B"
0476:  C0        RET   NZ         No, then end
0477:  2C        INC   L          third character will be
0478:  7E        LD    A,(HL)     checked
0479:  FE 4D     CP    $4D        against "M"
047B:  C0        RET   NZ         No, not a Boot sector
047C:  2E FF     LD    L,$FF      Counter on last character
047E:  7E        LD    A,(HL)     Get this character
047F:  C9        RET              and end the routine


********************************* error tread

0480:  CD 26 05   CALL  $0526     Output the following Text
0483:  93 05     .Byte $93,$05    line 19, column 5
```

```
0485:  33 32 4B 20 4D 41 58 20     32K MA:
048D:  43 50 4D 2B 2E 53 59 53     CPM+.SYS
0495:  20 53 49 5A 45 00           SIZE<End>
049B:  CF          RST   $08       Repeat Boot proceedings
049C:  3C          INC   A         Test if Accu=&FF
049D:  28 FC       JR    Z,$049B   If Accu=&FF also reboot
049F:  3A 36 3C    LD    A,($3C36) Else get the read counter
04A2:  3D          DEC   A         and decrement by one
04A3:  32 36 3C    LD    ($3C36),A put it down again
04A6:  20 AC       JR    NZ,$0454  Try again
04A8:  CD 26 05    CALL  $0526     Output the following text
04AB:  93 05       .Byte $93,$05   line 19, column 5
04AD:  52 45 41 44 20 45 52        READ ER
04B4:  52 4F 52 00                 ROR<End>
04B8:  CD 26 05    CALL  $0526     Output following text
04BB:  20 2D 20 48 49 54 20 52     HIT
04C5:  45 54 55 52 4E 20 54 4F     RETURN TO
04CD:  20 52 45 54 52 59           RETRY
04D1:  94 0F       .Byte $94,$0F   line $14,$0F
04D3:  44 45 4C 20 54 4F 20 45     DEL TO E
04DB:  4E 54 45 52 20 43 31 32     ENTER C128
04E3:  38 20 4D 4F 44 45 00        MODE<End>
04EA:  01 00 DC    LD    BC,$DC00  Port A CIA1
                                   (Keyboard decoding)
04ED:  3E FE       LD    A,$FE     DEL- and <CR> are
04EF:  ED 79       OUT   (C),A     masked and checked
04F1:  0C          INC   C         Pointer to Port B of CIA1
04F2:  ED 78       IN    A,(C)     Get result
04F4:  E6 02       AND   $02       Test Bit for <CR>
04F6:  28 A3       JR    Z,$049B   <CR> was hit -> Reboot
04F8:  ED 78       IN    A,(C)     Else get new value
04FA:  E6 01       AND   $01       Test DEL-Bit
04FC:  20 EC       JR    NZ,$04EA  Not hit, then keep trying
04FE:  C7          RST   $00       Else in the  C-128-Mode
04FF:  CD 26 05    CALL  $0526     Output the following text
0502:  93 05       .Byte $93,$05   line  19, column 5
0504:  4E 4F 00                    NO<End>
0507:  CD 26 05    CALL  $0526     Output the following text
050A:  20 43       .Byte $20,$43   $20=Ab Cursor position
050B:  43 50 4D 2B 2E 53 59 53     CPM+.SYS
0513:  20 46 49 4C 45 00           FILE<End>
0519:  18 9D       JR    $04B8     New try or 128 Mode
051B:  CD 26 05    CALL  $0526     Output the following text
```

```
051E:  93          .Byte $93,$05   Line  $13, column $05
0520:  42 41 44 00                 BAD<End>
0524:  18 E1       JR    $0507     New try or 128-Mode


******************************** Output the following text

0526:  E3          EX    (SP),HL   return address from Stack
0527:  CD 34 05    CALL  $0534     Output text from HL to$00
052A:  E3          EX    (SP),HL   End of Text as new return
052B:  C9          RET             address  and RETurn


********************************* Output text from DE

052C:  21 FF FF    LD    HL,$FFFF  character mask for output
052F:  22 04 24    LD    ($2404),  Set character
0532:  D5          PUSH  DE        Text address  to Stack
0533:  E1          POP   HL        and read in HL


********************************* Output text from HL

0534:  56          LD    D,(HL)    Get  character
0535:  23          INC   HL        Increment pointer to
                                   Text position
0536:  3A 05 24    LD    A,($2405  Get mask
0539:  A7          AND   A         Set flags
053A:  28 05       JR    Z,$0541   Mask allows everything,
                                   end
053C:  AA          XOR   D         Otherwise string together
                                   with mask
053D:  32 05 24    LD    ($2405),  and write back
0540:  57          LD    D,A       character to D
0541:  7A          LD    A,D       actual character
0542:  B7          OR    A         Set flags
0543:  C8          RET   Z         Zero character signals end
0544:  FE 24       CP    $24       Dollar sign?
0546:  C8          RET   Z         If yes, then end
0547:  E5          PUSH  HL        Save the actual counter
0548:  21 33 05    LD    HL,$0533  jump from address  $0533
054B:  E5          PUSH  HL        simulate
054C:  FE 0A       CP    $0A       If line feed, then
```

```
054E:  C8         RET    Z          return on this address
054F:  FE 0D      CP     $0D        Is character <CR>?
0551:  20 0B      JR     NZ,$055    No, then to $055E
0553:  CD 45 0A   CALL   $0A45      column=0 - 40 characters
0556:  CD F1 06   CALL   $06F1      column=0 - 80 characters
0559:  CD F1 09   CALL   $09F1      Increment line pointer
055C:  DF         RST    $18        jump to $06D1 (Increment
                                    line counter)
055D:  0C         .Byte  $0C        Return vector
055E:  FE FF      CP     $FF        Ist character $FF?
0560:  20 17      JR     NZ,$0579   No, then jump over
                                    erasing part
0562:  11 00 18   LD     DE,$1800   Pointer to Status line
                                    (line /column)
0565:  CD 85 05   CALL   $0585      Set Cursor position
0568:  CD 48 0A   CALL   $0A48      Erase status line  (40er)
056B:  CD 7A 07   CALL   $077A      Erase status line  (VDC)
056E:  11 00 00   LD     DE,$0000   Pointer to first
                                    screen position
0571:  CD 85 05   CALL   $0585      Set Cursor position
0574:  CD 62 0A   CALL   $0A62      Erase cursor position to
                                    screen end
0577:  DF         RST    $18        The same for VDC
0578:  20         .Byte  $20        Return vector 32
0579:  E6 80      AND    A,$80      Test Bit 7
057B:  28 39      JR     Z,$05B6    If erased,then output
                                    normal character
057D:  C1         POP    BC         Simulate  RS-address  back
057E:  E1         POP    HL         Pointer back
057F:  5E         LD     E,(HL)     Get column
0580:  23         INC    HL         Pointer to next character
0581:  E5         PUSH   HL         Save pointer
0582:  C5         PUSH   BC         Save simulated
                                    CALL-address
0583:  CB BA      RES    7,D        Erase bit 7 from line
0585:  D5         PUSH   DE         Save  line /column
0586:  CD BC 09   CALL   $09BC      Set 40-character-Cursor
0589:  D1         POP    DE         Get  line /column
058A:  DF         RST    $18        Jump on
                                    80-character-Cursor
058B:  04         .Byte  $04        Return vector is 4
```

```
*********************************Announce block
                                 (Track/sector) to read

058C:  11 4A 18   LD    DE,$184A  Set line  24,
                                  column 74 as Cursor
058F:  CD AB 06   CALL  $06AB     Set 80-char cursor pos.
0592:  11 22 18   LD    DE,$1822  Line  24, column 34
0595:  CD BC 09   CALL  $09BC     Set 40-character-Cursor
0598:  3A 03 FD   LD    A,($FD0   to read  track
059B:  CD A6 05   CALL  $05A6     wander in ASCII
059E:  16 20      LD    D,$20     Blank character
05A0:  CD B6 05   CALL  $05B6     output
05A3:  3A 04 FD   LD    A,($FD0   to loading sector


********************************* Make out <Accu> ASCII

05A6:  06 2F      LD    B,$2F     ASCII "0" - 1
05A8:  04         INC   B         Increment ten's place
05A9:  D6 0A      SUB   $0A       Move (if possible) 10 down
05AB:  30 FB      JR    NC,$05A8  Ten's place is still
                                  not zero
05AD:  C6 3A      ADD   A,$3A     error correction plus
                                  ASCII "0"
05AF:  F5         PUSH  AF        Save one's place
05B0:  78         LD    A,B       Ten's place (ASCII)
                                  to <Accu>
05B1:  CD B5 05   CALL  $05B5     and output
05B4:  F1         POP   AF        Get one's place (ASCII)


********************************* Output character <accu)

05B5:  57         LD    D,A       characters after <D>
05B6:  D5         PUSH  DE        and note
05B7:  CD 6E 09   CALL  $096E     character output
05BA:  D1         POP   DE        Get output character (V)
05BB:  DF         RST   $18       character to
                                  40-character-screen
05BC:  00         .Byte $00       Vector 0
```

```
******************************** Prepare 80 character set

05BD:  21 04 30  LD    HL,$3004  Address  in VDC-RAM
05C0:  CD 3D 09  CALL  $093D     Get value from $3004
05C3:  04        INC   B         and check against 0 by
05C4:  05        DEC   B         decrementing and
                                 incrementing
05C5:  C8        RET   Z         If zero, then it was
                                 already prepared
05C6:  21 00 38  LD    HL,$3800  Fill $3800 to
05C9:  01 00 04  LD    BC,$0400  $3FFF with the
05CC:  16 00     LD    D,$00     value 0
05CE:  CD 47 08  CALL  $0847     (erase)
05D1:  21 A0 37  LD    HL,$37A0  ASCII 122
05D4:  11 A0 38  LD    DE,$38A0  becomes
05D7:  01 08 00  LD    BC,$0008  ASCII 138
05DA:  CD B0 08  CALL  $08B0
05DD:  21 90 36  LD    HL,$369   ASCII 105
05E0:  11 90 38  LD    DE,$3890  becomes
05E3:  01 08 00  LD    BC,$0008  ASCII 137
05E6:  CD B0 08  CALL  $08B0
05E9:  21 E0 35  LD    HL,$35E0  ASCII 94 (PI)
05EC:  11 E0 38  LD    DE,$38E0  becomes
05EF:  01 18 00  LD    BC,$0018  ASCII 95 (_)
05F2:  CD B0 08  CALL  $08B0
05F5:  21 10 30  LD    HL,$3010  A-Z (ASCII 1-26)
05F8:  11 10 36  LD    DE,$3610  to
05FB:  01 98 01  LD    BC,$0198  ASCII 97 ff.
05FE:  CD B0 08  CALL  $08B0
0601:  21 00 30  LD    HL,$300   Erase $3000 to $31FF
0604:  01 00 02  LD    BC,$0200  in
0607:  16 00     LD    D,$00     VDC-RAM
0609:  CD 47 08  CALL  $0847
060C:  21 00 20  LD    HL,$2000  Copy "@" (ASCII 64)
060F:  11 00 34  LD    DE,$3400  into  VDC-
0612:  01 08 00  LD    BC,$0008  RAM
0615:  CD B0 08  CALL  $08B0
0618:  21 B0 21  LD    HL,$21B0  t to u (ASCII 27 thru 29)
061B:  11 B0 35  LD    DE,$35B   to
061E:  01 28 00  LD    BC,$0028  ASCII 91
0621:  CD B0 08  CALL  $08B0
0624:  21 C0 21  LD    HL,$21C0  ASCII 28 (find character)
0627:  11 00 38  LD    DE,$3800  to
```

```
062A:  01 08 00   LD     BC,$0008   ASCII 128
062D:  CD B0 08  CALL    $08B0
0630:  21 E0 21   LD     HL,$21E0  ASCII 30 (^) becomes 129
0633:  11 10 38   LD     DE,$3810  and
0636:  01 18 00   LD
0639:  CD B0 08   CALL   $08B0
063C:  21 00 24   LD     HL,$2400  Capital letters and
                                   other characters
063F:  11 00 3C   LD     DE,$3C00  to $3C00 (ASCII 192)
0642:  01 F8 03   LD     BC,$03F8
0645:  CD B0 08   CALL   $08B0
0648:  11 1A 0F   LD     DE,$0F1A  ASCII 227
064B:  21 C0 35   LD     HL,$35C   becomes
064E:  CD 70 06   CALL   $0670     ASCII 92
0651:  21 E0 35   LD     HL,$35    ASCII 228-230
0654:  06 03      LD     B,$03     becomes
0656:  CD 62 06   CALL   $0662     ASCII 94-96
0659:  21 B0 37   LD     HL,$37B   ASCII 231-235
065C:  06 05      LD     B,$05     becomes
065E:  18 02      JR     $0662     ASCII 123 ff.
0660:  E1         POP    HL        Get return address to HL
0661:  E3         EX     (SP),HL   and erase a return address


********************************** Copy (DE)->(HL) VDC (BC)

0662:  C5         PUSH   BC        Save counter
0663:  E5         PUSH   HL        Note destination address
0664:  CD 70 06   CALL   $0670     (DE)->(HL) VDC-RAM  8
                                   Bytes
0667:  E1         POP    HL        Get goal address  back
0668:  01 10 00   LD     BC,$001   And add 16 (instead of 8)
066B:  09         ADD    HL,BC     because of internal
                                   VDC-building
066C:  C1         POP    BC        Get counter back
066D:  10 F3      DJNZ   $0662     Another character to copy?
066F:  C9         RET              No, then end
```

```
******************************** (DE)->(HL) VDC; 8 Bytes


0670:  CD 53 0    CALL  $0953      Announce HL as update
0673:  26 08      LD    H,$08      8 Bytes should be copied
0675:  1A         LD    A,(D       Get the character from RAM
0676:  ED 79      OUT   (C),A      and store it in VDC
0678:  0D         DEC   C          Pointer to Status-Flag
0679:  13         INC   DE         Increment pointer to table
067A:  ED 78      IN    A,(C)      Get status flag
067C:  17         RLA              Test ready-Bit
067D:  30 FB      JR    NC,$067    Still not finished
067F:  0C         INC   C          Pointer again to $D601
0680:  25         DEC   H          Decrement pointer
0681:  20 F2      JR    NZ,$06     and jump if still not
                                   8 Bytes
0683:  C9         RET              else end routine

******************************** Output <A> character inkl.
                                   Cursormove


0684:  2A 11 24   LD    HL,($2411 Get cursor address
0687:  CD 07 09   CALL  $0907      Output character on
                                   80-character
068A:  3A 13 24   LD    A,($241    Cursor column
068D:  FE 4F      CP    $4F        right boarder
                                   (79) reached?
068F:  28 3C      JR    Z,$06CD    Yes, then next  line
0691:  3C         INC   A          else increment the
                                   column pointer
0692:  32 13 24   LD    ($2413),   and note the new column
0695:  2A 11 24   LD    HL,($241   Get  cursor address
0698:  23         INC   HL         and also increment a place
0699:  22 11 24   LD    ($2411), H  and store again


******************************** Set HL as Cursor address

069C:  3E 0E      LD    A,$0E      Cursor address  Hi-Byte
069E:  CD 45 09   CALL  $0945      Announce to VDC
06A1:  ED 61      OUT   (C),H      Hand over High Byte on VDC
```

```
06A3:  3E 0F      LD    A,$0F        Register 15 is
                                     Cursor address  Lo
06A5:  CD 45 09   CALL  $0945        announce to VDC
06A8:  ED 69      OUT   (C),L        and also pass Lo-Byte
06AA:  C9         RET                End of transfer


********************************* Set 80-character-Cursor
                                     position
                                     D:column, E: line

06AB:  7A         LD    A,D          Get  line
06AC:  FE 19      CP    $19          Larger than 24
06AE:  D0         RET   NC           Yes, then invalid and end
06AF:  7B         LD    A,E          Get column
06B0:  FE 50      CP    $50          Larger than 79?
06B2:  D0         RET   NC           Yes, then invalid and end
06B3:  EB         EX    DE,HL        for the purpose of storing
                                     HL to DE
06B4:  22 13 24   LD    ($2413),HL    and noting
                                      Cursor position
06B7:  2A 13 24   LD    HL,($2413) Get cursor position
06BA:  CD CE 0C   CALL  $0CCE         line *80 + column
06BD:  22 11 2    LD    ($2411),HL Note address
06C0:  18 DA      JR    $069C         Pass cursor address
                                      to VDC


********************************* Decrement line  by one

06C2:  3A 14 24   LD    A,($2414) Get cursor line
06C5:  B7         OR    A            set the CPU-Flags
06C6:  C8         RET   Z            Line is already the
                                     then stop
06C7:  3D         DEC   A            else decrement the  line
06C8:  32 14 24   LD    ($2414),A and note this
06CB:  18 EA      JR    $06B7        new calculated
                                     cursor address
```

```
********************************* Column=0 (1st col)
                                  set inkl.
                                  Influence lines

06CD:  AF        XOR   A          Accu becomes null
06CE:  32 13 24  LD    ($2413),A   and note as column
06D1:  3A 14 24  LD    A,($241    Get actual cursor line
06D4:  FE 17     CP    $17        Is it the 23rd line.?
06D6:  28 21     JR    Z,$06F     Reached, then jump
06D8:  30 1A     JR    NC,$06F4   Line  is 24
06DA:  3C        INC   A          Else increment line
                                  by one
06DB:  18 EB     JR    $06C8      and  mark line


********************************* Decrement column by one

06DD:  3A 13 2   LD    A,($2413   Get actual column
06E0:  B7        OR    A          set flags to test for zero
06E1:  C8        RET   Z          If already first column,
                                  then end
06E2:  3D        DEC   A          else decrement column pter
06E3:  32 13 24  LD    ($2413),A   and note new column
06E6:  18 CF     JR    $06B7      Calculate new
                                  Cursor address


********************************* Increment column by one

06E8:  3A 13 24  LD    A,($2413)  Get actual column
06EB:  3C        INC   A          and increment by one
06EC:  FE 50     CP    $50        has column 80 been
                                  reached?
06EE:  20 F3     JR    NZ,$06E    No, then mark column
06F0:  C9        RET              else end the routine


********************************* Set column to 0
                                  (first column)

06F1:  AF        XOR   A          Set accu to exactly 0,
06F2:  18 EF     JR    $06E3      then note as new column
```

```
********************************** Set line =23

06F4:  3E 17      LD    A,$17       Set line  to 23rd
06F6:  32 14 24   LD    ($2414),A    and mark in memory
06F9:  21 50 00   LD    HL,$0050    Scroll the screen
06FC:  11 00 00   LD    DE,$0000    one  line   up
06FF:  01 30 07   LD    BC,$0730    by copying the 2nd line to
0702:  CD B0 08   CALL  $08B0       the first line  etc.
0705:  21 30 07   LD    HL,$0730    Pointer to last line  (not
                                    Status line )
0708:  01 50 00   LD    BC,$0050    Number is 80 characters
070B:  CD 41 08   CALL  $0841       Line  erase
070E:  18 A7      JR    $06B7       announce new cursor
                                    position


********************************** Define new
                                    attributes(B:to erase,
                                    C:to set parameters)

0710:  3A 15 24   LD    A,($2415)   Get attribute
0713:  2F         CPL               Complement attribute
0714:  B0         OR    B           to erase Bits (qualities)
0715:  2F         CPL               complement again
0716:  B1         OR    C           to set Bits (qualities)
0717:  32 15 24   LD    ($2415),A   Store the new attributes
071A:  C9         RET               Routine's end


**********************************

071B:  78         LD    A,B         Get character
071C:  D6 20      SUB   $20         Subtract ASCII 32 (blank)
071E:  FE 20      CP    $20         ASCII 32?
0720:  38 0A      JR    C,$072C     Smaller, then jump
0722:  0E 20      LD    C,$20       Move marker for ASCII 32
0724:  CD E5 0C   CALL  $0CE5       Transform ASCII + Code
0727:  D8         RET   C           Produce
0728:  7E         LD    A,(HL)      Get character from table
0729:  E6 0F      AND   $0F         Mask Bits 4-7
072B:  80         ADD   A,B         and mark <B> as Offset
072C:  32 00 24   LD    ($2400)     character
```

```
072F:  0E 20     LD    C,$20      ASCII 32
                                  subtraction-counter
0731:  C6 30     ADD   A,$30      ASCII 48 ("0") add
0733:  21 0A 0F  LD    HL,$0F0A   Table for color alteration
0736:  CD E8 0C  CALL  $0CE8      transform
0739:  7E        LD    A,(HL)     Get color values
073A:  80        ADD   A,B        and add attribute
073B:  FE 10     CP    $10        Transfer into high
                                  value Nibble?
073D:  38 1B     JR    C,$075A    Foreground color
                                  is defined
073F:  E6 0F     AND   $0F        else mask Bits 4-7
0741:  32 16 24  LD    ($2416),A  Note background color
0744:  F5           PUSH  AF      Save color code
0745:  3E 1A        LD    A,$1A   Register
                                  26=fore/background
                                  color
0747:  CD 45 09  CALL  $0945      VDC-Status wait for
                                  and announce
074A:  F1        POP   AF         Get color value
074B:  ED 79     OUT   (C),A      and set color
074D:  C9        RET              End of the routine


********************************* B:Backgnd, D:Attribut
                                  A:Foregnd

074E:  3A 16 24  LD    A,($2417)  Get background color
0751:  47        LD    B,A        and move to <B>
0752:  3A 15 24  LD    A,($2415)  Get attribute
0755:  57        LD    D,A        and move to D
0756:  3A 17 24  LD    A,($2417)  Get foreground color
0759:  C9        RET              End of the routine


*********************************Define new foreground color

075A:  47        LD    B,A        Color to B
075B:  3A 15 24  LD    A,($2417)  Get actual attribute
075E:  E6 F0     AND   $F0        Mask color nibble
0760:  B0        OR    B          and set a new color
0761:  32 15 24  LD    ($2415),A  note new attribute
0764:  3A 00 24  LD    A,($2400)  Get background color and
```

```
0767:   32 17 24   LD     ($2417),A note
076A:   2A 11 24   LD     HL,($2411 Get Cursor address
076D:   11 00 08   LD     DE,$0800  Offset for RAM attribute
0770:   19         ADD    HL,DE     add
0771:   CD 53 09   CALL   $0953     Announce HL as Update
0774:   3A 15 24   LD     A,($241)  Get attribute
0777:   ED 79      OUT    (C),A     store to Cursor address
0779:   C9         RET              End of routine


********************************** Erase cursor position to
                                    line end

077A:   CD C7 0C   CALL   $0CC7     Get cursor position,
                                    number of characters
077D:   03         INC    BC        Increment the number
077E:   18 0E      JR     $078E     erase the rest of the line


********************************* Erase Cursor position to
                                  screen's end

0780:   CD C7 0C   CALL   $0CC7     Get Cursor position,
                                    number of character
0783:   EB         EX     DE,HL     Cursor address  to DE
0784:   21 80 07   LD     HL,$0780  address beginning of
                                    status line
0787:   AF         XOR    A         Erase carry for
                                    subtraction
0788:   ED 52      SBC    HL,DE     Calculate # chars to
                                    status line
078A:   F8         RET    M         If negative, then
                                    End (error)
078B:   44         LD     B,H       Else BC exactly
078C:   4D         LD     C,L       Number characters to
                                    status line
078D:   EB         EX     DE,HL     and actual cursor position
                                    again to HL
078E:   C3 41 08   JP     $0841     Erase to beginning of
                                    status line
```

```
******************************** Insert 1 character shift
                                 rest line

0791:  CD C7 0C   CALL  $0CC7     Get cursor position and
                                  number character
0794:  21 4F 00   LD    HL,$004F  add 79 to line beginning
0797:  19         ADD   HL,DE     go to line beginning
0798:  3D         DEC   A         Number chars to line end-1
0799:  28 2C      JR    Z,$07C7   Nothing more then stop
079B:  54         LD    D,H       Address the line end
079C:  5D         LD    E,L       to DE
079D:  2B         DEC   HL        Address  line end-1
079E:  C5         PUSH  BC        Save number
079F:  E5         PUSH  HL        Save source
07A0:  D5         PUSH  DE        Save destination
07A1:  CD AD 07   CALL  $07AD    Copy (HL)->(DE) in VDC-RAM
07A4:  01 00 08   LD    BC,$0800 Now add Offset for
07A7:  E1       POP   HL         RAM attribute in VDC
07A8:  09       ADD   HL,BC  To  source address
07A9:  EB       EX    DE,HL      note in DE get
07AA:  E1       POP   HL         destination address
                                 from Stack
07AB:  09       ADD   HL,BC      also add the offset
07AC:  C1       POP   BC         get number
07AD:  C5       PUSH  BC         and save again
07AE:  CD 53 0 CALL  $0953       Announce HL as update
07B1:  ED 78    IN    A,(C)      Get actual contents
07B3:  EB       EX    DE,HL      Exchange destination and
                                 goal address
07B4:  F5       PUSH  AF         Save the found
                                 out character
07B5:  CD 53    CALL  $095       Announce HL again
                                 as update
07B8:  F1       POP   AF         Get back the found
                                 out character
07B9:  ED 79    OUT   (C),A      copy in destination
                                 address
07BB:  EB       EX    DE,HL      Goal and destination
                                 addresses again ok.
07BC:  C1       POP   BC         Get number back
07BD:  2B       DEC   HL         Decrement source pointer
07BE:  1B       DEC   DE         Decrement destination
                                 pointer
```

```
07BF:  0B         DEC   BC        Decrement the counter
07C0:  78         LD    A,B       Make sure Register-
07C1:  B1         OR    C         pair BC is exactly zero
07C2:  20 E9      JR    NZ,$07AD then copy next character
07C4:  2A 11 24   LD    HL,($2411) else get Cursor address,
07C7:  C3 05 09   JP    $0905     output a blank character


********************************* Erase character in Cursor
                                  position

07CA:  CD C7 0C   CALL  $0CC7     Get Cursor address  and
                                  number of characters
07CD:  D5         PUSH  DE        Save line beginning
                                  to stack
07CE:  54         LD    D,H       actual Cursor position
07CF:  5D         LD    E,L       copy to DE
07D0:  23         INC   HL        Increment source by one
07D1:  CD B0 08   CALL  $08B0     (HL)->(DE) BC times =
                                  erase one character
07D4:  E1         POP   HL        Line beginning to HL
07D5:  11 4F 00   LD    DE,$004F  And add 79 for
07D8:  19         ADD   HL,DE     line end
07D9:  C3 05 09   JP    $0905     Output a blank char to
                                  end line


********************************* Insert a  line on
                                  cursor line


07DC:  11 62 0F   LD    DE,$0F6   Pointer to table
07DF:  3E 17      LD    A,$17     Line  23 in accu
07E1:  2A 13 24   LD    HL,($2413) Get line /column
07E4:  BC         CP    H         Line  23 reached?
07E5:  CA 05 07   JP    Z,$0705   Yes, then erase 23rd line
07E8:  38 1A      JR    C,$0804   smaller than 23, then jump
07EA:  21 E0 06   LD    HL,$06E0  Source address  (third to
                                  last  line )
07ED:  11 30 07   LD    DE,$0730  Destination address
                                   (second to last line )
07F0:  06 18      LD    B,$18     24  lines are to be copied
07F2:  CD 0A 08   CALL  $080A     Copy line  (HL) to (DE)
```

```
07F5:  3A 14 24   LD    A,($2414) Get  line
07F8:  B8         CP    B         Actual line reached?
07F9:  20 F7      JR    NZ,$07F2  No, then continue copying
07FB:  CD C7 0C   CALL  $0CC7     Get cursor position and
                                  # characters
07FE:  EB         EX    DE,HL     HL: line beginning
07FF:  01 50 00   LD    BC,$0050  80 as beginning of the
                                  following lines
0802:  18 3D      JR    $0841     Erase cursor line
0804:  3C         INC   A         This location won't be
0805:  BD         CP    L         reached, or the cursor
0806:  C0         RET   NZ        would be on status line
0807:  C3 2C 05   JP    $052C     Output text from DE


******************************    Copy line (HL) to (DE)
                                  in VDC

080A:  C5         PUSH  BC        Save number to stack
080B:  E5         PUSH  HL        Save source addr to stack
080C:  D5         PUSH  DE        Save destination address
                                   to  stack
080D:  01 50 00   LD    BC,$0050  80 characters per line
0810:  CD B0 08   CALL  $08B0     Copy line
0813:  01 B0 FF   LD    BC,$FFB0  Adding 80's complement is
                                  used for subtraction
0816:  E1         POP   HL        Get destination address
0817:  09         ADD   HL,BC     delete  80 characters
0818:  EB         EX    DE,HL     and put into  DE
0819:  E1         POP   HL        Get source address
081A:  09         ADD   HL,BC     subtract 80
081B:  C1         POP   BC        Get number
081C:  05         DEC   B         Decrement the counter
081D:  C9         RET             End of the routine


******************************    Erase cursor line and move
                                  the rest up

081E:  3A 14 24   LD    A,($2414)Get line
0821:  FE 18      CP    $18       Has line 24 been reached?
0823:  D0         RET   NC        Yes, then quit
```

```
0824:  CD C7 0C   CALL  $0CC7     Get cursor pos and
                                  number of chars
0827:  21 50 00   LD    HL,$0050  Add 80 to the start address
082A:  19         ADD   HL,DE     of the cursor line
082B:  EB         EX    DE,HL     and note that in DE
082C:  E5         PUSH  HL        Push start address to
                                  the Stack
082D:  21 80 07   LD    HL,$0780  Status line's start address
0830:  AF         XOR   A         Erase carry for subtraction
0831:  ED 52      SBC   HL,DE     Subtract the following
                                  line's start add
0833:  44         LD    B,H       Give the number of
                                  characters up to the
0834:  4D         LD    C,L       screen's end to BC
0835:  E1         POP   HL        Get start address back

0836:  EB         EX    DE,HL     Exchange source and
                                   destination address
0837:  CD B0 08   CALL  $08B0     (HL)->(DE) in VDC-RAM
083A:  C3 05 07   JP    $0705     Erase the last line before
                                  the stat line


******************************    Put value in VDC-RAM

083D:  E1         POP   HL        Get return address
083E:   E3        EX    (SP),HL   and exchange  with
                                  preceding return address
083F:  18 06      JR    $0847     Jump to routine
0841:  3A 15 24   LD    A,($2415) Get attribute
0844:  5F         LD    E,A       Load attribute into E
0845:  16 20      LD    D,$20     ASCII-Code for blank char


****************************** Fill (HL) in VDC-RAM with
                                  D,attribute with E
                                  (HL+800) will be filled.
0847:  78         LD    A,B       Test number's Hi-Byte
0848:  A7         AND   A         and Hi-Byte against zero
0849:  28 0D      JR    Z,$0858   If zero, then only fill
                                  Lo-Byte
084B:  E5         PUSH  HL        Save destination address
084C:  D5         PUSH  DE        Save fill values
```

```
084D:  C5          PUSH  BC        Save number
084E:  AF          XOR   A         Accu=0 means 256 character
084F:  CD 5B 08    CALL  $085B     Fill (HL) with D, 256 times
0852:  C1          POP   BC        Get number back
0853:  D1          POP   DE        Get fill values back
0854:  E1          POP   HL        Get destnation address back
0855:  24          INC   H         Increment Hi-Byte
0856:  10 F3       DJNZ  $084B     If bigger than 256
                                   character, then jump
0858:  79          LD    A,C       Test Lo-Byte against
0859:  A7          AND   A         zero (nothing more to fill)
085A:  C8          RET   Z         and end, if done


*****************************      Save character <D> to <HL>
                                   <a> number of  times

085B:  F5          PUSH  AF        Save number
085C:  E5          PUSH  HL        Save destination address
085D:  D5          PUSH  DE        Save fill character
085E:  CD 6C 08    CALL  $086C     Save character D
0861:  D1          POP   DE        Get fill character
0862:  01 00 08    LD    BC,$0800  Offset for RAM attribute
0865:  E1          POP   HL        Retrieve destination
                                   address
0866:  09          ADD   HL,BC     and add Offset
0867:  CD FE 08    CALL  $08FE     See if HL is a
                                   legitimate address
086A:  F1          POP   AF        If ok, get counter
086B:  53          LD    D,E       and attribute as fill char


*****************************      character <D> <A> times to
                                   <HL> in VDC-RAM

086C:  F5          PUSH  AF        Save counter to stack
086D:  CD 53 09    CALL  $0953     Announce HL as update
0870:  ED 51       OUT   (C),D     and pass character
0872:  F1          POP   AF        Get number from stack
0873:  3D          DEC   A         Decrement the counter
0874:  C8          RET   Z         and end if full enough
0875:  F5          PUSH  AF        else save counter
0876:  3E 18       LD    A,$18     Announce Register 24
```

```
0878:  CD 45 09   CALL  $0945     (copy-bit)
087B:  ED 78      IN    A,(C)     Get register's contents
087D:  E6 7F      AND   $7F       and mask copy-Bit
087F:  ED 79      OUT   (C),A     Again into VDC memory
0881:  3E 1E      LD    A,$1E     Select register 31
                                  (Word count)
0883:  CD 45 09   CALL  $0945     and announce
0886:  F1         POP   AF        Get number from Stack
0887:  ED 79      OUT   (C),A     and pass the number's
                                  remainder to VDC
0889:  06 00      LD    B,$00     Set BC's Hi-Byte to zero
088B:  4F         LD    C,A       and Lo-Byte with
                                  number's remainder
088C:  03         INC   BC        add one
088D:  09         ADD   HL,BC     add start address
088E:  D5         PUSH  DE        Save start address
088F:  E5         PUSH  HL        Save calculated stop addr
0890:  3E 12      LD    A,$12     Update Hi-Byte-Register
0892:  CD 45 09   CALL  $0945     announce
0895:  ED 60      IN    H,(C)     and read the entire value
0897:  3E 13      LD    A,$13     Update Lo-Byte-Register
0899:  CD 45 09   CALL  $0945     announce
089C:  ED 68      IN    L,(C)     and read the entire value
089E:  D1         POP   DE        Get the calculated
                                  stop address
089F:  C1         POP   BC        Get start address
08A0:  CD FA 00   CALL  $00FA     Compare HL with DE
08A3:  D0         RET   NC        Everything OK, no mistakes!
08A4:  C5         PUSH  BC        Number to Stack
08A5:  CD 53 09   CALL  $0953     Announce HL as Update
08A8:  C1         POP   BC        Get number's remainder
08A9:  ED 41      OUT   (C),B     and error correction
08AB:  23         INC   HL        if calculated stop address
08AC:  18 F2      JR    $08A0     and actual stop address are
                                  different
08AE:  E1         POP   HL        Get return address
08AF:  E3         EX    (SP),HL   and go one deeper in
                                  the Stack
```

```
****************************** (HL) -> (DE) in VDC-RAM
                                 <BC> times

08B0:  78        LD    A,B       Get number's Hi-Byte
08B1:  A7        AND   A         Test Hi-Byte against zero
08B2:  28 0E     JR    Z,$08C2   If zero, then number<256
08B4:  E5        PUSH  HL        Save source address
08B5:  D5        PUSH  DE        Save destination address
08B6:  C5        PUSH  BC        Save number toStack
08B7:  AF        XOR   A         erase Accu for 256 chars
08B8:  CD C5 08  CALL  $08C5     (HL)->(DE) <A> times
08BB:  C1        POP   BC        Get number
08BC:  D1        POP   DE        Get destination address
08BD:  E1        POP   HL        Get source address
08BE:  24        INC   H         Increment source address'
                                 Hi-Byte
08BF:  14        INC   D         Increment destination
                                 address' Hi-Byte
08C0:  10 F2     DJNZ  $08B4     If more than 256 character,
08C2:  79        LD    A,C       then get Lo-number
08C3:  A7        AND   A         see if it is zero
08C4:  C8        RET   Z         end if it is zero
08C5:  EB        EX    DE,HL     else exchange source and
                                 destination addresses
08C6:  F5        PUSH  AF        Save number to Stack
08C7:  E5        PUSH  HL        Save destination address
08C8:  D5        PUSH  DE        Save source address
08C9:  CD D8 08  CALL  $08D8     (DE)->(HL) in VDC-RAM
                                 <A> number of times
08CC:  01 00 08  LD    BC,$0800  Offset for RAM attribute
08CF:  E1        POP   HL        Get source address
08D0:  09        ADD   HL,BC     add Offset
08D1:  EB        EX    DE,HL     Source address+Offset
                                 into DE
08D2:  E1        POP   HL        Get destination address
08D3:  09        ADD   HL,BC     add Offset
08D4:  CD FE 08  CALL  $08FE     Test against memory
                                 boundary
08D7:  F1        POP   AF        Get number
```

```
*****************************  (DE) -> (HL) in
                               VDC-accumulator
                               <A> times

08D8:  F5         PUSH  AF     Save number to stack
08D9:  CD 53 09   CALL  $0953  Announce HL as
                               Update address
08DC:  3E 18      LD    A,$18  Announce register 24
08DE:  CD 45 09   CALL  $0945  (copy bit)
08E1:  ED 78      IN    A,(C)  Get register's contents
08E3:  F6 80      OR    $80    and set the copybit
08E5:  ED 79      OUT   (C),A  Report register to VDC
08E7:  3E 20      LD    A,$20  Announce Register 32
                               (Block-Start-Hi)
08E9:  CD 45 09   CALL  $0945  in VDC
08EC:  ED 51      OUT   (C),D  Pass Hi-address source
08EE:  3E 21      LD    A,$21  Announce Register 33
                               (Block-Start-Lo)
08F0:  CD 45 09   CALL  $0945  in VDC
08F3:  ED 59      OUT   (C),E  and pass Lo-address source
08F5:  3E 1E      LD    A,$1E  Announce Register 31 (Word
08F7:  CD 45 09   CALL  $0945  count)
08FA:  F1         POP   AF     and get number from stack
08FB:  ED 79      OUT   (C),A  Report VDC number
08FD:  C9         RET          End of routine


*****************************  Test if after adding the
                               offset <HL>
                               the RAM attribute changes

08FE:  7C         LD    A,H    Load Hi-Byte into accu
08FF:  FE 20      CP    $20    and check the border
0901:  D8         RET   C      If carry is set, <HL> is OK
0902:  F1         POP   AF     Get AF from stack
0903:  F1         POP   AF     Get return address from
                               the Stack
0904:  C9         RET          and a return occurs after
                               CALL $085B
```

```
******************************  Output blank character to
                                (HL)  (VDC)

0905:  16 20     LD    D,$20     ASCII value for <space>
0907:  3A 15 24  LD    A,($2415) Get attribute


******************************  Output character <D> with
                                attribute <A> to (HL)

090A:  E5        PUSH  HL        Save destination address
090B:  D5        PUSH  DE        Save character/attribute
090C:  11 00 08  LD    DE,$0800 Add offset for RAM
                                 attribute
090F:  19        ADD   HL,DE     to destination address
0910:  57        LD    D,A       Output attribute as
                                 the fill character
0911:  CD 16 09  CALL  $0916    <D> to  (HL)
0914:  D1        POP   DE        Get character
0915:  E1        POP   HL        Get destination address
0916:  CD 53 09  CALL  $0953     Use HL as update
0919:  ED 51     OUT   (C),D     and output char to (HL)
091B:  C9        RET             Routine's end


******************************  Get <C>:attribute,
                                <B>:character, to
                                cursor position <DE>

091C:  CD AB 06  CALL  $06AB     Set cursor position <DE>
091F:  2A 11 24  LD    HL,($2411) Get cursor address
0922:  CD 33 09  CALL  $0933     Get character/attribute
0925:  4F        LD    C,A       <C> is attribute
0926:  C9        RET             End of the routine


******************************  <B>:character,
                                <C>:attribute, output
                                to <DE>

0927:  C5        PUSH  BC        Save character/attribute
0928:  CD AB 06  CALL  $06AB     Set cursor position <DE>
092B:  2A 11 24  LD    HL,($2411)Get Cursor address
```

```
092E:  C1        POP   BC        Get character/atrribute
092F:  50         LD    D,B      <D> is a character
0930:  79         LD    A,C      <A> is an attribute
0931:  18 D7     JR    $090A     Output character and
                                 attribute


******************************   Get <A>:Attribute,
                                 <B>:character to (HL)

0933:  E5        PUSH  HL        Save address
0934:  11 00 08  LD    DE,$0800  Add offset for
                                 attribute address
0937:  19        ADD   HL,DE
0938:  CD 3D 09  CALL  $093D     Get values to
                                 VDC-address (HL)
093B:  78        LD    A,B       Attribute to  <A>
093C:  E1        POP   HL        Get text address
093D:  F5        PUSH  AF        Save attribute
093E:  CD 53 09  CALL  $0953     Use (HL) as update
0941:  F1        POP   AF        Get attribute
0942:  ED 40     IN    B,(C)     Get value to address (HL)
0944:  C9        RET             Routine's end


******************************   Wait forVDC-Status

0945:  F5        PUSH  AF        Save output register
0946:  01 00 D6  LD    BC,$D600  Start address VDC-Chip
0949:  ED 78     IN    A,(C)     Get Status
094B:  17        RLA             Shift Status-Bit into Carry
094C:  30 FB     JR    NC,$0949  Still not done -> jump
094E:  F1        POP   AF        Get the register from stack
                                 once more
094F:  ED 79     OUT   (C),A     and choose register
0951:  0C        INC   C         Point to  $D601
0952:  C9        RET             and RETurn from routine
```

```
******************************   HL as Update-address

0953:  3E 12      LD    A,$12     Announce Update-address Hi
0955:  CD 45 09   CALL  $0945
0958:  ED 61      OUT   (C),H     Pass Hi-Byte
095A:  3E 13      LD    A,$13     Announce Update-address Lo
095C:  CD 45 09   CALL  $0945
095F:  ED 69      OUT   (C),L     Pass Lo-Byte
0961:  3E 1F      LD    A,$1F     Announce word count
                                  register
0963:  CD 45 09   CALL  $0945
0966:  0D         DEC   C         Pointer again to $D600
0967:  ED 78      IN    A,(C)     Get Status
0969:  17         RLA             Roll status into Carry
096A:  30 FB      JR    NC,$0967  Still not done
096C:  0C         INC   C         Yes now, pointer to $D601
096D:  C9         RET             RETurn from subroutine


******************************   Output character <D> to
                                  40-character screen

096E:  42         LD    B,D       character to <B>
096F:  CD 7F 0C   CALL  $0C7F     ASCII code transform VIC
0972:  2A 09 24   LD    HL,($2409)80-character-address
0975:  47         LD    B,A       character to <B>
0976:  3A 10 24   LD    A,($2410)Get character offset
                                  (Bit 7 1/0)
0979:  B0         OR    B         Operate with character
097A:  77         LD    (HL),A    and write into RAM
097B:  23         INC   HL        Increment pointer
097C:  22 09 24   LD    ($2409),HL and mark this
097F:  11 FF 07   LD    DE,$07FF  Add to offset
0982:  19         ADD   HL,DE     for color RAM
0983:  3A 0D 24   LD    A,($240D)Get character color
0986:  77         LD    (HL),A    and set character color
0987:  3A 0B 24   LD    A,($240B)Get cursor position
098A:  FE 4F      CP    $4F       Last column?
098C:  28 5F      JR    Z,$09ED   Yes, then jump lines
098E:  3C         INC   A         else increment the
                                  column pointer
098F:  32 0B 24   LD    ($240B),A and mark the new position
0992:  C3 4A 0C   JP    $0C4A     Represent line
```

```
******************************  Get character <B> and color
                                <C> from  Cursor pos (DE)

0995:  CD C1 09   CALL  $09C1    Define line/column (DE)
0998:  2A 09 24   LD    HL,($2409) Get cursor address of
                                80-character simulator
099B:  46         LD    B,(HL)   Get character in
                                Cursor position
099C:  11 00 08   LD    DE,$0800 Add offset for RAM
                                attribute
099F:  19         ADD   HL,DE
09A0:  4E         LD    C,(HL)   Get attribute in
                                Cursor position
09A1:  C9         RET            End of routine


******************************  <B>:character,<C>:attribute
                                to (DE)

09A2:  C5         PUSH  BC       Save character/attribute
09A3:  CD C1 09   CALL  $09C1    Set Cursor position
09A6:  C1         POP   BC       Get character/attribute
09A7:  2A 09 24   LD    HL,($2409) Get 80-character
                                simulator address
09AA:  78         LD    A,B      character into <Accu>
09AB:  E6 7F      AND   $7F      Erase Bit 7
09AD:  CB 71      BIT   6,C      Test Bit 6
09AF:  28 02      JR    Z,$09B3  Isn't set
09B1:  C6 80      ADD   A,$80    Set Bit 7 (reverses
                                character)
09B3:  77         LD    (HL),A   and set character
09B4:  11 00 08   LD    DE,$0800 Add offset for
                                RAM attribute
09B7:  19         ADD   HL,DE
09B8:  71         LD    (HL),C   Define attribute also
09B9:  C3 4A 0C   JP    $0C4A    Represent line


******************************  Def. line/column

09BC:  21 04 24   LD    HL,$2404 address 40-character
09BF:  CB F6      SET   6,(HL)   40-character bit set
09C1:  7A         LD    A,D      Get line
```

```
09C2:  FE 19     CP    $19       Bigger than 24?
09C4:  D0        RET   NC        Yes, then end (error)
09C5:  7B        LD    A,E       Get column
09C6:  FE  50    CP    $50       Have reached column 80?
09C8:  D0        RET   NC        Yes, then end (mistake)
09C9:  EB        EX    DE,HL     line/column to HL
09CA:  22 0B 24  LD    ($240B),HL Set line/column


****************************** New cursor position

09CD:  2A 0B 24  LD    HL,($240B Get line/column
09D0:  CD CE 0C  CALL  $0CCE     Calculate new cursor
                                 address
09D3:  11 00 14  LD    DE,$1400 Add offset for
                                 80-character simulator
09D6:  19        ADD   HL,DE     to it
09D7:  22 09 24  LD    ($2409),HL And note the
                                 adjusted address
09DA:  C3 4A 0C  JP    $0C4A     Represent line


****************************** Decrement line

09DD:  3A 0C 24  LD    A,($240C) Get cursor line
09E0:  B7        OR    A         Set Flags
09E1:  C8        RET   Z         line 0! Don't do anything
09E2:  3D        DEC   A         else decrement line pointer
09E3:  32 0C 24  LD    ($240C),A and note line
09E6:  21 04 24  LD    HL,$2404 Set Bit 6 to $2404
09E9:  CB F6     SET   6,(HL)    as OK-character
09EB:  18 E0     JR    $09CD     Calculate new
                                 cursor position


****************************** Column=0 Define column (+1)

09ED:  AF        XOR   A         Accu=0 for first column
09EE:  32 0B 24  LD    ($240B),A and define column
09F1:  3A 0C 24  LD    A,($240C) Get line
09F4:  FE 17     CP    $17       Last line?
09F6:  28 0A     JR    Z,$0A02   Yes, then jump
09F8:  30 03     JR    NC,$09FD Correct errors
```

```
09FA:  3C         INC   A          Increment line by one
09FB:  18 E6      JR    $09E3      and note
09FD:  3E 17      LD    A,$17      Note line 23 (last
09FF:  32 0C 24   LD    ($240C),A line)
0A02:  21 50 14   LD    HL,$1450   Second line's start address
0A05:  11 00 14   LD    DE,$1400   First line's start address
0A08:  01 30 07   LD    BC,$0730   Copy 22 lines
0A0B:  ED B0      LDIR             Scrolling
0A0D:  EB         EX    DE,HL      Destination address
                                   as source
0A0E:  11 31 1B   LD    DE,$1B31   Last line's 2nd character
0A11:  01 4F 00   LD    BC,$004F   Fill 79 characters
0A14:  CD 24 0B   CALL  $0B24      Fll last line with
                                   fill characters
0A17:  21 50 1C   LD    HL,$1C50   Second line's address
                                   beginning (attribute)
0A1A:  11 00 1C   LD    DE,$1C00   1st line's address
                                   beginning (attribute)
0A1D:  01 30 07   LD    BC,$0730   Scroll 22 lines
0A20:  ED B0      LDIR   Execute scrolling in color RAM
0A22:  EB         EX    DE,HL      1st char of last line to HL
0A23:  11 31 23   LD    DE,$2331   2nd character of last line
                                   (color RAM)
0A26:  01 4F 00   LD    BC,$004F   Fill 79 characters
0A29:  3A 0D 24   LD    A,($240D) Get color for color RAM
0A2C:  77         LD    (HL),A     set
0A2D:  ED B0      LDIR   and also fill the rest of the line
0A2F:  18 B5      JR    $09E6      OK set


******************************  Move cursor left

0A31:  3A 0B 24   LD    A,($240B) Get column position
0A34:  B7         OR    A          Set Flags
0A35:  C8         RET   Z          First column? Then end
0A36:  3D         DEC   A          else move cursor left
0A37:  32 0B 24   LD    ($240B),A Store the new column
0A3A:  18 91      JR    $09CD      Calculate cursor address
```

```
******************************   Move cursor right

0A3C:  3A 0B 24   LD    A,($240B) Get column
0A3F:  3C         INC   A         and move it right
0A40:  FE 50      CP    $50       Have we reached the
                                  80th column?
0A42:  20 F3      JR    NZ,$0A37 No, then store the
                                  new position
0A44:  C9         RET             else don't move the cursor


******************************   Set column = 0

0A45:  AF         XOR   A         Erase accu and
0A46:  18 EF      JR    $0A37     store as column value


******************************   Erase from cursor position
                                  to line end

0A48:  21 CF 0B   LD    HL,$0BCF Return after
0A4B:  E5         PUSH  HL        simulating $0BCF
0A4C:  CD C2 0C   CALL  $0CC2     Find out cursor pos and
                                  rest of chars/line
0A4F:  11 00 14   LD    DE,$1400 Add offset for
                                  80-character simulator
0A52:  19         ADD   HL,DE
0A53:  CD B3 0A   CALL  $0AB3     Set fill characters
0A56:  79         LD    A,C       rest of characters/line
0A57:  A7         AND   A         Set Flags
0A58:  C8         RET   Z         No more characters
0A59:  C5         PUSH  BC        Save number
0A5A:  E5         PUSH  HL        Save source address
0A5B:  54         LD    D,H       Register pair DE
0A5C:  5D         LD    E,L       equals HL
0A5D:  13         INC   DE        plus 1
0A5E:  ED B0      LDIR            Erase up to line end
0A60:  18 1C      JR    $0A7E     Also erase attribute
```

```
******************************  Erase from cursor pos to
                                end of screen

0A62:  21 0C 0C  LD    HL,$0C0C Simulate $0C0C as
                                return address
0A65:  E5        PUSH  HL       for the stack
0A66:  11 7F 1B  LD    DE,$1B7F The last line's last column
0A69:  2A 09 24  LD    HL,($2409) Get cursor address
                                80-character-Simulator
0A6C:  EB        EX    DE,HL    to DE, $1B7F to HL
0A6D:  AF        XOR   A        Erase carry for subtraction
0A6E:  ED 52     SBC   HL,DE    Find # of chars to
                                end of screen
0A70:  F8        RET   M        if negative, there is error
0A71:  EB        EX    DE,HL    else give result to DE
0A72:  28 3F     JR    Z,$0AB3  If only one char, then fill
0A74:  42        LD    B,D      else number
0A75:  4B        LD    C,E      into register pair BC
0A76:  54        LD    D,H      and register pair DE
                                (destination)
0A77:  5D        LD    E,L      equals register pair HL
0A78:  13        INC   DE       plus one
0A79:  C5        PUSH  BC       Push number to Stack
0A7A:  E5        PUSH  HL       Push source onto Stack
0A7B:  CD 24 0B  CALL  $0B24    Fill text line with
                                attribute
0A7E:  01 00 08  LD    BC,$0800 Offset for color RAM
0A81:  E1        POP   HL       Retrieve source address
0A82:  09        ADD   HL,BC    and add offset
0A83:  C1        POP   BC       Get number of characters
0A84:  54        LD    D,H      Destination address equals
0A85:  5D        LD    E,L      source address
0A86:  13        INC   DE       plus one
0A87:  3A 0D 24  LD    A,($240D) Get color for
                                color RAM VIC
0A8A:  77        LD    (HL),A   and set color
0A8B:  ED B0     LDIR           fill the rest up
                                to screen's end
0A8D:  C9        RET            End of the routine
```

```
******************************   Insert one space at
                                 the cursor position

0A8E:  21 CF 0B  LD    HL,$0BCF Copy line from RAM
                                 to screen
0A91:  E5        PUSH  HL        as return address for Stack
0A92:  CD C2 0C  CALL  $0CC2     Find out cursor pos and
                                 rest of character
0A95:  21 4F 14  LD    HL,$144F Add the last char of the
                                 first line
0A98:  19        ADD   HL,DE     to the cursor address
0A99:  3D        DEC   A         last column?
0A9A:  28 17     JR    Z,$0AB3   Yes, then jump
0A9C:  54        LD    D,H       Else destination goal is =
0A9D:  5D        LD    E,L       source address
0A9E:  2B        DEC   HL        minus one
0A9F:  C5        PUSH  BC        Save number to stack
0AA0:  D5        PUSH  DE        Save destination address
                                 to Stack
0AA1:  ED B8     LDDR            Move char behind Curs right
0AA3:  EB        EX    DE,HL     HL:=Cursor pos
0AA4:  CD B3 0A  CALL  $0AB3     Get fill characters
0AA7:  E1        POP   HL        Retrieve destination addr
0AA8:  01 00 08  LD    BC,$0800 Add offset for color RAM
0AAB:  09        ADD   HL,BC     to source address
0AAC:  C1        POP   BC        Retrieve number
0AAD:  54        LD    D,H       Destination address equals
0AAE:  5D        LD    E,L       source address
0AAF:  2B        DEC   HL        minus one
0AB0:  ED B8     LDDR            Move color RAM also
0AB2:  C9        RET             End of the routine


******************************   ($2410) + $20 -> (HL); set
                                 the fill characters

0AB3:  3A 10 24  LD    A,($2410) read address $2410
                                 (Fill characters)
0AB6:  C6 20     ADD   A,$20     Add $20=32 tp ot
0AB8:  77        LD    (HL),A    and store in (HL)
0AB9:  C9        RET             RETurn from routine
```

```
******************************  Erase a character in
                                Cursor position

0ABA:  21 CF 0B  LD    HL,$0BCF Give $0BCF as return
                                address to stack
0ABD:  E5        PUSH  HL       insert extra
0ABE:  CD C2 0C  CALL  $0CC2    Get cursor address/
                                rest of characters
0AC1:  11 00 14  LD    DE,$1400 Add offset for
                                80-character simulator
0AC4:  19        ADD   HL,DE    to Cursor address
0AC5:  3D        DEC   A        Test number/character
0AC6:  28 EB     JR    Z,$0AB3  If zero, then jump
0AC8:  54        LD    D,H      else destination address =
0AC9:  5D        LD    E,L      source address
0ACA:  C5        PUSH  BC       Save number
0ACB:  E5        PUSH  HL       Save source address
0ACC:  23        INC   HL       Source address is equal to
                                source address+1
0ACD:  ED B0     LDIR   Erase   char in cursor position
0ACF:  EB        EX    DE,HL    Cursor address to HL
0AD0:  CD B3 0A  CALL  $0AB3    Set fill character
0AD3:  E1        POP   HL   Get source address
0AD4:  01 01 08  LD    BC,$0801 Add offset for color RAM+1
0AD7:  09        ADD   HL,BC
0AD8:  C1        POP   BC       Get # of chars from Stack
0AD9:  54        LD    D,H      Destination address equals
0ADA:  5D        LD    E,L      source address
0ADB:  23        INC   HL       plus one
0ADC:  ED B0     LDIR           Also move color RAM
0ADE:  C9        RET            End of routine


******************************  Insert 1 line at
                                cursor position

0ADF:  21 0C 0C  LD    HL,$0C0C Insert return address $0C0C
0AE2:  E5        PUSH  HL       push to stack
0AE3:  3A 0C 24  LD    A,($240C) Get cursor line
0AE6:  FE 17     CP    $17      line 23 (last)?
0AE8:  28 31     JR    Z,$0B1B  Yes, then just erase
0AEA:  D0        RET   NC       Mistake, then end
0AEB:  CD C2 0C  CALL  $0CC2    Get cursor address/
```

```
                                     rest of characters
0AEE:  21 00 14   LD    HL,$1400  Add offset for
                                     80-character simulator
0AF1:  19         ADD   HL,DE     to it
0AF2:  E5         PUSH  HL        Save source address
                                     to stack
0AF3:  11 50 00   LD    DE,$0050  Add offset for the
                                     beginning of the next
0AF6:  19         ADD   HL,DE     to start address
0AF7:  EB         EX    DE,HL     Result to (DE)
0AF8:  21 80 1B   LD    HL,$1B80  Last line's address
0AFB:  AF         XOR   A         Erase carry for subtraction
0AFC:  ED 52      SBC   HL,DE     Find out number chars to
                                     end of screen
0AFE:  44         LD    B,H       Number comes from
0AFF:  4D         LD    C,L       HL to BC
0B00:  21 2F 1B   LD    HL,$1B2F  last column of
                                     second-to-last line
0B03:  11 7F 1B   LD    DE,$1B7F  last column of last line
0B06:  C5         PUSH  BC        Save number to stack
0B07:  ED B8      LDDR            Insert a line on
                                     the cursor line
0B09:  C1         POP   BC        Retrieve number
0B0A:  21 2F 23   LD    HL,$232F  Color RAM's address
0B0D:  11 7F 23   LD    DE,$237F  Color RAM's address
0B10:  ED B8      LDDR            also move
0B12:  E1         POP   HL        Get source address
0B13:  54         LD    D,H       DE equals
0B14:  5D         LD    E,L       source address
0B15:  13         INC   DE        plus one
0B16:  01 4F 00   LD    BC,$004F  79 characters
0B19:  18 09      JR    $0B24     Erase new line
0B1B:  21 30 1B   LD    HL,$1B30  Only erase the last
0B1E:  11 31 1B   LD    DE,$1B31  line
0B21:  01 4F 00   LD    BC,$004F  because cursor is
                                     on last line
0B24:  3A 10 24   LD    A,($2410)  Get fill character
0B27:  C6 20      ADD   A,$20     add 32 ( blank character)
0B29:  77         LD    (HL),A    and set fill character
0B2A:  ED B0      LDIR            fill the rest with
                                     fill characters
0B2C:  C9         RET             and end the routine
```

```
******************************   Erase cursor line
                                 and move screen

0B2D:  21 0C 0C  LD    HL,$0C0C Push return address $0C0C
0B30:  E5        PUSH  HL       to stack
0B31:  3A 0C 24  LD    A,($240C)Get cursor line
0B34:  FE 17     CP    $17      Last line?
0B36:  28 E3     JR    Z,$0B1B  Yes, then only erase
                                the last line
0B38:  D0        RET   NC       On NC error and end
0B39:  CD C2 0C  CALL  $0CC2    Calculate cursor address/
                                rest of chars
0B3C:  21 00 14  LD    HL,$1400 Add offset for
                                80-character simulator
0B3F:  19        ADD   HL,DE    to cursor address
0B40:  E5        PUSH  HL       Save source address to stak
0B41:  11 50 00  LD    DE,$0050 Add offset for start of
0B44:  19        ADD   HL,DE    the following line
0B45:  EB        EX    DE,HL    Result to DE
0B46:  21 80 1B  LD    HL,$1B80 address status line
0B49:  AF        XOR   A        Erase carry for subtraction
0B4A:  ED 52     SBC   HL,DE    Find number of chars to
                                end of screen
0B4C:  44        LD    B,H      number
0B4D:  4D        LD    C,L      to BC
0B4E:  EB        EX    DE,HL    Start address->HL
0B4F:  D1        POP   DE       Get Start addr cursor line
0B50:  C5        PUSH  BC       Save number to stack
0B51:  E5        PUSH  HL       Save source addres to stack
0B52:  D5        PUSH  DE       Save goal address to stack
0B53:  ED B0     LDIR           and erase line
0B55:  01 00 08  LD    BC,$0800 Add offset for color RAM
0B58:  E1        POP   HL       to the
0B59:  09        ADD   HL,BC    source address
0B5A:  EB        EX    DE,HL    Result to DE
0B5B:  E1        POP   HL       Get start address of
                                second-to-last line of
                                color RAM
0B5C:  09        ADD   HL,BC    also add offset
0B5D:  C1        POP   BC       Get number
0B5E:  ED B0     LDIR           and also move color RAM
0B60:  18 B9     JR    $0B1B    Erase last line
```

```
******************************   <B>:off, <C>:turned on Bits
                                 of character color

0B62:  78        LD    A,B       Turned on Bits to <A>
0B63:  E6 70     AND   $70       Erase Bit 7 und Bits 0-3
0B65:  47        LD    B,A       Result to <B>
0B66:  79        LD    A,C       Get the set Bits
0B67:  E6 70     AND   $70       Also erase bits0,1,2,3,4,7
0B69:  4F        LD    C,A       Result to C
0B6A:  3A 0D 24  LD    A,($240D) Get attribute complement
0B6D:  2F        CPL             set to
0B6E:  B0        OR    B         erased characteristics
0B6F:  2F        CPL             complement again and
0B70:  B1        OR    C         set to set characteristics
0B71:  32 0D 24  LD    ($240D),A Note the new attribute
0B74:  17        RLA             shift 6th Bit into 7th
0B75:  E6 80     AND   $80       Reverse char and mask
0B77:  32 10 24  LD    ($2410),A Values $00 thru $80 as
                                 fill characters
0B7A:  C9        RET             End of routine


******************************

0B7B:  78        LD    A,B       Get output chars to<Accu>
0B7C:  D6 20     SUB   $20       Minus ASCII 32
0B7E:  FE 30     CP    $30       smaller than 48?
0B80:  38 0E     JR    C,$0B90   Yes, then jump
0B82:  0E 30     LD    C,$30     else note 48 as the number
0B84:  CD E5 0C  CALL  $0CE5     further coding
0B87:  D8        RET   C         Everything clear
0B88:  7E        LD    A,(HL)    Get color
0B89:  0F        RRCA  /2
0B8A:  0F        RRCA  /2=/4
0B8B:  0F        RRCA  /2=/8
0B8C:  0F        RRCA  /2=/16
0B8D:  E6 0F     AND   $0F       Masks Bits 4-7
0B8F:  80        ADD   A,B       and add <B> to it again
0B90:  FE 10     CP    $10       Transfer into the high
                                 value Nibble?
0B92:  38 29     JR    C,$0BBD   No, define new color
0B94:  FE 20     CP    $20       Frame or background color ?
0B96:  38 0B     JR    C,$0BA3   Define background color
```

```
******************************  Set frame color

0B98:  E6 0F     AND   $0F       Mask Bits 7-4
0B9A:  32 0F 24  LD    ($240F),A and note frame color
0B9D:  01 20 D0  LD    BC,$D020  Address for frame color
0BA0:  ED 79     OUT   (C),A     Pass frame color to VIC
0BA2:  C9        RET             End of routine


******************************  Set background color for
                                 40-character

0BA3:  E6 0F     AND   $0F       Mask Bits 4-7
0BA5:  32 0E 24  LD    ($240E),A and note background color
0BA8:  01 21 D0  LD    BC,$D021 Address for background color
0BAB:  ED 79     OUT   (C),A    Pass background color to VIC
0BAD:  C9        RET             End of routine


******************************  Get: <B>:background,
                                 <C>:frame,
                                 <D>:character color

0BAE:  3A 0E 24  LD    A,($240E)Get background color
0BB1:  47        LD    B,A       note in <B>
0BB2:  3A 0F 24  LD    A,($240F)Get frame
0BB5:  4F        LD    C,A       Note in <C>
0BB6:  3A 0D 24  LD    A,($240D)Get char color
0BB9:  57        LD    D,A       Note in <D>
0BBA:  E6 0F     AND   $0F       Mask unimportant bits 7-4
0BBC:  C9        RET             End of routine


******************************  Define new color

0BBD:  47        LD    B,A       Code to <B>
0BBE:  3A 0D 24  LD    A,($240D)Get old color
0BC1:  E6 F0     AND   $F0       Get Bits 0 to 3
0BC3:  B0        OR    B         and new color
0BC4:  32 0D 24  LD    ($240D),A Store new color
0BC7:  2A 09 24  LD    HL,($2409)Get cursor address
0BCA:  11 00 08  LD    DE,$0800  Add offset for
                                 RAM attribute
```

```
0BCD:  19        ADD   HL,DE
0BCE:  77        LD    (HL),A     Set new color


******************************     Copy line from RAM
                                   to screen

0BCF:  3A 04 24  LD    A,($2404)Marker for output
0BD2:  47        LD    B,A        into <B>
0BD3:  B7        OR    A          Set Flags
0BD4:  FC 3C 0C  CALL  M,$0C3C    If bit 7 is set,
                                  then pay attention
0BD7:  3A 02 24  LD    A,($2402)Get column considered
0BDA:  B8        CP    B          equal to 80-char column?
0BDB:  32 04 24  LD    ($2404),A mark column
0BDE:  20 2C     JR    NZ,$0C0C different, then jump
0BE0:  CD C2 0C  CALL  $0CC2      Calculate cursor position
0BE3:  21 00 14  LD    HL,$1400 Add offset $1400
0BE6:  19        ADD   HL,DE
0BE7:  EB        EX    DE,HL      and mark in DE
0BE8:  2A 02 24  LD    HL,($2402)add the column
                                  being considered
0BEB:  19        ADD   HL,DE      gives destination address
0BEC:  E5        PUSH  HL         save to stack
0BED:  3A 0C 24  LD    A,($240C) Get line
0BF0:  6F        LD    L,A        and into <L>
0BF1:  CD 70 0C  CALL  $0C70      Calculate line start
                                  for 40-char
0BF4:  EB        EX    DE,HL      and note in DE
0BF5:  E1        POP   HL         Get address considered
0BF6:  E5        PUSH  HL         and save again
0BF7:  D5        PUSH  DE         save line beginning
0BF8:  3E 01     LD    A,$01      Copy 1 line
0BFA:  CD 27 0C  CALL  $0C27      Copy ($1400+SP) to screen
0BFD:  E1        POP   HL         40-character address back
0BFE:  01 00 E4  LD    BC,$E400 Offset for color RAM
0C01:  09        ADD   HL,BC      Add offset
0C02:  EB        EX DE,HL         and note in DE
0C03:  E1        POP   HL         Get source address
0C04:  01 00 08  LD    BC,$0800 Offset screen color RAM
0C07:  09        ADD   HL,BC      Add to source address
0C08:  3E 01     LD    A,$01      1 line
0C0A:  18 1B     JR    $0C27      and copy
```

```
******************************* Copy 40-character screen

0C0C:  2A 02 24  LD    HL,($2402)Get cursor address
0C0F:  3A 08 24  LD    A,($2408) Number represented
                                 character/line
0C12:  E5        PUSH  HL        save Cursor address
0C13:  F5        PUSH  AF        save number/character
0C14:  11 00 14  LD    DE,$1400  Add offset for 80-character
                                 simulation
0C17:  19        ADD   HL,DE
0C18:  11 00 2C  LD    DE,$2C00  Videoram
0C1B:  CD 27 0C  CALL  $0C27     Copy line
0C1E:  F1        POP   AF        Get number
0C1F:  E1        POP   HL        Get source address
0C20:  11 00 1C  LD    DE,$1C00  Add offset for color RAM
0C23:  19        ADD   HL,DE
0C24:  11 00 10  LD    DE,$1000  color RAM address
                                 (being considered)


******************************* (HL) -> (DE) 40 characters
                                 in screen <A> lines

0C27:  32 03 FF  LD    ($FF03),A PCRC as configuration's
                                 byte
0C2A:  01 28 00  LD    BC,$0028 Copy 40 characters
0C2D:  ED B0     LDIR           (HL) -> (DE)
0C2F:  D5        PUSH  DE       Save destinationaddress
0C30:  11 28 00  LD    DE,$0028 40-characters to be copied
0C33:  19        ADD   HL,DE    add to source address
0C34:  D1        POP   DE       Get destination address
0C35:  3D        DEC   A        Decrement the counter
0C36:  20 F2     JR    NZ,$0C2A one more line to copy
0C38:  32 01 FF  LD    ($FF01),A else PCRA as
                                 configuration's byte
0C3B:  C9        RET            End of the routine


******************************* Paying attention to column

0C3C:  3A 0B 24  LD    A,($240B)Get column
0C3F:  D6 20     SUB   $20      minus 32
0C41:  30 01     JR    NC,$0C44 No transfers occur
```

```
0C43:  AF        XOR   A          else erase accu (=0)
0C44:  E6 F8     AND   $F8        Mask Bits 0-2
0C46:  32 02 24  LD    ($2402),A Note the column
                                  being considered
0C49:  C9        RET              End of the routine


****************************** Copy line

0C4A:  CD 69 0C  CALL  $0C69      Erase $2406
0C4D:  CD CF 0B  CALL  $0BCF      Copy line
0C50:  3A 02 24  LD    A,($2402) Get column being considered

0C53:  47        LD    B,A        Write in <B>
0C54:  2A 0B 24  LD    HL,($240B)Get line/column
0C57:  7D        LD    A,L        column into <A> for
                                  subtraction
0C58:  90        SUB   B          minus column being
                                  considered
0C59:  38 0E     JR    C,$0C69    too small, then erase $2406
0C5B:  FE 28     CP    $28        too big--bigger than 40?
0C5D:  30 0A     JR    NC,$0C69   then erase $2406
0C5F:  4F        LD    C,A        column into <C>
0C60:  06 00     LD    B,$00      Erase Hi-Byte from BC
0C62:  6C        LD    L,H        <L>=line
0C63:  CD 70 0C  CALL  $0C70      And calculate line's
                                  Start address
0C66:  09        ADD   HL,BC      add column
0C67:  18 03     JR    $0C6C      and note the address
0C69:  21 00 00  LD    HL,$0000   Start address is
                                  1st Position
0C6C:  22 06 24  LD    ($2406),HL note the Position
0C6F:  C9        RET              End of the routine


****************************** line*40 + Offset

0C70:  26 00     LD    H,$00      Erase Hi-Byte
0C72:  29        ADD   HL,HL      *2
0C73:  29        ADD   HL,HL      *2
0C74:  29        ADD   HL,HL      *2=*8
0C75:  54        LD    D,H        write to DE
0C76:  5D        LD    E,L
```

```
0C77:  29         ADD   HL,HL      *2
0C78:  29         ADD   HL,HL      *2=*32
0C79:  19         ADD   HL,DE      *32+*8 gives *40
0C7A:  11 00 2C   LD    DE,$2C00   Add offset from $2C00
0C7D:  19         ADD   HL,DE      (beginning of text)
0C7E:  C9         RET              End of the routine


********************************   Adapting ASCII-Code
                                    for 40-character screen

0C7F:  78         LD    A,B        character into <accu>
0C80:  FE 40      CP    $40        Is it ASCII 64 (@)
0C82:  28 3C      JR    Z,$0CC0    Yes, then Poke-Code=0
0C84:  D8         RET   C          If smaller, then end
0C85:  FE 5B      CP    $5B        smaller than ASCII "Z"+1?
0C87:  D8         RET   C          Yes, then return
0C88:  D6 40      SUB   $40        Subtract 64
0C8A:  FE 20      CP    $20        Is it an apostrophe?
0C8C:  28 19      JR    Z,$0CA7    Yes, then code
0C8E:  38 23      JR    C,$0CB3    smaller than an apostrophe
0C90:  D6 20      SUB   $20        minus ASCII 32
0C92:  FE 1B      CP    $1B        small letter's boarder
0C94:  D8         RET   C          Smaller, then end
0C95:  FE 1B      CP    $1B        compare again
0C97:  28 11      JR    Z,$0CAA    small ASCII "{"?
0C99:  FE 1C      CP    $1C        small "|"?
0C9B:  28 10      JR    Z,$0CAD    Yes, then code
0C9D:  FE 1D      CP    $1D        small "}"?
0C9F:  28 0F      JR    Z,$0CB0    Yes, then code
0CA1:  FE 1E      CP    $1E        Is it "~"?
0CA3:  C0         RET   NZ         No, then return
0CA4:  3E 40      LD    A,$40      else code 64
0CA6:  C9         RET              End of the routine


********************************   ASCII-Code 126

0CA7:  3E 7E      LD    A,$7E      126
0CA9:  C9         RET              End of the routine
```

```
******************************* ASCII-Code 115

0CAA:  3E 73     LD    A,$73     115
0CAC:  C9        RET             End of the routine


******************************* ASCII-Code 93

0CAD:  3E 5D     LD    A,$5D     93
0CAF:  C9        RET             End of the routine


******************************* ASCII-Code 107

0CB0:  3E 6B     LD    A,$6B     107
0CB2:  C9        RET             End of the routine


******************************* ASCII-Code 28

0CB3:  FE 1C     CP    $1C       ASCII 28?
0CB5:  28 06     JR    Z,$0CBD   Yes, then assign
0CB7:  FE 1F     CP    $1F       ASCII 31?
0CB9:  C0        RET   NZ        No, then end with Flag
0CBA:  3E 64     LD    A,$64     Else ASCII 100
0CBC:  C9        RET             End of the routine


******************************* Assign ASCII-Code 127

0CBD:  3E 7F     LD    A,$7F     127
0CBF:  C9        RET             End of the routine


******************************* Erase <accu>

0CC0:  AF        XOR   A         Erase <Accu>
0CC1:  C9        RET             End of the routine
```

```
******************************** Calculate <C>:79-column
                                 and Cursorpos.


0CC2:  2A 0B 24  LD    HL,($240B)Get line/column
0CC5:  18 03     JR    $0CCA     continue

0CC7:  2A 13 24  LD    HL,($2413)Get line/column
0CCA:  3E 4F     LD    A,$4F     integer 79
0CCC:  95        SUB   L         minus column
0CCD:  4F        LD    C,A       Note in <C> (other numbers
                                 until 80)

******************************** Calculate cursor position
                                 <H>:line, <L>:column


0CCE:  45        LD    B,L       <B> equals column
0CCF:  6C        LD    L,H       <L> is now line
0CD0:  26 00     LD    H,$00     Erase Hi-Byte
0CD2:  29        ADD   HL,HL     *2
0CD3:  29        ADD   HL,HL     *2
0CD4:  29        ADD   HL,HL     *2
0CD5:  29        ADD   HL,HL     *2=*16
0CD6:  54        LD    D,H       <DE> will be occupied by
0CD7:  5D        LD    E,L       line times 16
0CD8:  29        ADD   HL,HL     *2
0CD9:  29        ADD   HL,HL     *2 gives *64
0CDA:  19        ADD   HL,DE     plus *16 gives *80
0CDB:  EB        EX    DE,HL     line times 80 into <DE>
0CDC:  68        LD    L,B       column into <L>
0CDD:  26 00     LD    H,$00     Erase Hi-Byte
0CDF:  19        ADD   HL,DE     and add line*80
0CE0:  06 00     LD    B,$00     Erase Hi-Byte from <BC>
0CE2:  3C        INC   A         <A>:=actual number of
                                 possible characters
0CE3:  C9        RET             End of the routine


******************************** ASCII-Decoding Cont'd

0CE4:  78        LD    A,B       character to <Accu>
0CE5:  2A 0D FD  LD    HL,($FD0D)Table pointer
0CE8:  D6 30     SUB   $30       Minus ASCII 48 "0"
```

```
0CEA:   D8          RET    C         Smaller, then end
0CEB:   B9          CP     C         Else compare w/ <C>
                                      (value taken off)
0CEC:   3F          CCF              Negate Carry-Flag
0CED:   D8          RET    C         and end if greater than or =
0CEE:   47          LD     B,A       Else character into <B>
0CEF:   E6 0F       AND    $0F       Mask Bits 0-3
0CF1:   5F          LD     E,A       Lo-Byte equals <Accu>
0CF2:   16 00       LD     D,$00     and erase Hi-Byte
0CF4:   19          ADD    HL,DE     add to table basis
0CF5:   78          LD     A,B       character again into <Accu>
0CF6:   E6 30       AND    $30       Mask Bits 6,7 and 0-3
0CF8:   47          LD     B,A       character again into <B>
0CF9:   C9          RET              End of the routine


******************************** Ringing out the tone

0CFA:   01 18 D4    LD     BC,$D418 SID Register 24
0CFD:   2A 10 FD    LD     HL,($FD10)Get Attack/Decay/Volume
0D00:   ED 61       OUT    (C),H     Total loudness
                                      strength/Filter
0D02:   0E 05       LD     C,$05     Define Register 5  SID:
0D04:   ED 69       OUT    (C),L     Attack/Decay
0D06:   2A 12 FD    LD     HL,($FD12)Get Sustain/
                                      Release/Frequency
0D09:   0C          INC    C         Register 6 of SID
0D0A:   ED 61       OUT    (C),H     Define Sustain/Release
0D0C:   0E 01       LD     C,$01     Register 1 of SID: Frequency
0D0E:   ED 69       OUT    (C),L     Define Frequency (HI)
0D10:   2A 14 FD    LD     HL,($FD14)Get turn off/on
0D13:   0E 04       LD     C,$04     Register 4 of SID
0D15:   ED 61       OUT    (C),H     Turning on the tone
0D17:   ED 69       OUT    (C),L     Erase Bit to Sustain
0D19:   C9          RET              End of tone ringing routine


******************************** Will be copied to $1100

0D1A:   1100: A9 00       LDA #$00    Set configuration byte
0D1C:   1102: 8D 00 FF    STA $FF00   (all ROM)
0D1F:   1105: 6C FC FF    JMP ($FFFC)Reset the C-128-Mode
```

```
********************************* Will be copied to $3000
                                  Read a disk block

0D22: 3000: A9 00      LDA #$00   Still aren't
0D24: 3002: 8D 06 FD   STA $FD06  any errors
0D27: 3005: 20 11 30   JSR $3011  Load the Block
0D2A: 3008: 78         SEI        Interrupt handicap
0D2B: 3009: A9 3E      LDA #$3E   RAM and System I/O
0D2D: 300B: 8D 00 FF   STA $FF00  as configuration byte
0D30: 300E: 4C D0 FF   JMP $FFD0  and turn on Z-80
0D33: 3011: D8         CLD        Erase decimal flag
0D34: 3012: AD 01 FD   LDA $FD01  Set flag for vectors
0D37: 3015: D0 21      BNE $3038  erased?
0D39: 3017: A2 00      LDX #$00   Turn on ROM and System I/O
0D3B: 3019: 8E 00 FF   STX $FF00
0D3E: 301C: 8E 1A D0   STX $D01A  Erase IMR im VIC-Chip
0D41: 301F: A2 63      LDX #$63   Start up routine's Lo-Byte
0D43: 3021: A0 31      LDY #$31   and Hi-Byte the same
0D44: 3023: 8E 14 03   STX $0314  Lo-Byte as IRQ-Routine
0D48: 3026: 8C 15 03   STY $0315  Hi-Byte as IRQ-Routine
0D4B: 3029: 8E 16 03   STX $0316  Lo-Byte as BRK-Routine
0D4E: 302C: 8C 17 03   STY $0317  Hi-Byte as BRK-Routine
0D51: 302F: 8E 18 03   STX $0318  Lo-Byte as NMI-Routine
0D54: 3032: 8C 19 03   STY $0319  Hi-Byte as NMI-Routine
0D57: 3035: 4C D7 30   JMP $30D7  Continue on $30D7


********************************* Read form Block
                                  (Track/Sector) and
                                  load in memory

0D5A: 3038: AD 18 FD   LDA $FD18  Copy Lo-Byte's
                                  destination address
0D5D: 303B: 85 20      STA $20    to $20 and
0D5F: 303D: AD 19 FD   LDA $FD19  Hi-Byte's destination addr
0D62: 3040: 85 21      STA $21    to $21
0D64: 3042: AD 03 FD   LDA $FD03  Get track
0D67: 3045: 8D BF 31   STA $31BF  and copy in disk command
0D6A: 3048: 20 78 31   JSR $3178  Make out of <Accu>
                                   ASCII "xx"
0D6D: 304B: 8E B1 31   STX $31B1  Ten's place Track and
0D70: 304E: 8D B0 31   STA $31B0  one's place Track in
                                   command line
```

```
0D73: 3051: AD 04 FD  LDA $FD04   Get sector number
0D76: 3054: 8D BE 31  STA $31BE   Pass sector number for FSD
0D79: 3057: 20 78 31  JSR $3178   and wander in ASCII
0D7C: 305A: 8E AE 31  STX $31AE   Ten's place sector; also
0D7F: 305D: 8D AD 31  STA $31AD   one's place in command line
0D82: 3060: AD 08 FD  LDA $FD08   Test, if channel was opened
0D85: 3063: D0 2B     BNE $3090   No, then jump to $3090
0D87: 3065: 8D 00 FF  STA $FF00   Set config byte on (ROM)
0D8A: 3068: A2 0B     LDX #$0B    Define channel # 11 as
0D8C: 306A: 20 C6 FF  JSR $FFC6   input channel
0D8F: 306D: B0 16     BCS $30A7   On error to $30A7
0D91: 306F: 20 CC FF  JSR $FFCC   CLRCH; I/O normal again
0D94: 3072: 20 31 31  JSR $3131   Read Track/Sector
0D97: 3075: 20 99 31  JSR $3199   Channel 11 (#) as
                                   input channel
0D9A: 3078: A0 00     LDY #$00    Y-Index to zero
0D9C: 307A: 20 CF FF  JSR $FFCF   BASIN; get char from floppy
0D9F: 307D: 91 20     STA ($20),Y and put character in RAM
0DA1: 307F: C8        INY         next Byte
0DA2: 3080: D0 F8     BNE $307A   End still not reached
0DA4: 3082: 4C CC FF  JMP $FFCC   CLRCH; I/O normal again
0DA7: 3085: A9 FF     LDA #$FF    Block can't be gotten
0DA9: 3087: 2C        .Byte $2C   Skip; jump the
                                   following command
0DAA: 3088: A9 0D     LDA #$0D    Recognition char for error
0DAC: 308A: 8D 06 FD  STA $FD06   Set step
0DAF: 308D: 4C 08 30  JMP $3008   In Z-80 section again


******************************** Read data from file

0DB2: 3090: A9 00     LDA #$00    Set ROM and System I/O as
0DB4: 3092: 8D 00 FF  STA $FF00   config byte
0DB7: 3095: A2 0F     LDX #$0F    Logical File number 15
0DB9: 3097: 20 C9 FF  JSR $FFC9   Error channel as
                                   output channel
0DBC: 309A: B0 EC     BCS $3088   jump on error
0DBE: 309C: A0 06     LDY #$06    Output 6 chars
0DC0: 309E: B9 BC 31  LDA $31BC,Y Get chars from table
0DC3: 30A1: 20 D2 FF  JSR $FFD2   Output chars through
                                   error channel
0DC6: 30A4: 88        DEY         Next character
0DC7: 30A5: D0 F7     BNE $309E   Output further characters
```

```
0DC9: 30A7: 20 CC FF  JSR $FFCC  CLRCH; I/O normal again
0DCC: 30AA: 2C 0D DC  BIT $DC0D  Test ICR
0DCF: 30AD: AE BD 31  LDX $31BD  Number of data blocks
0DD2: 30B0: 20 4F 31  JSR $314F  Get Data byte (Fast-mode)
0DD5: 30B3: 29 0E     AND #$0E   Test Bits 1-3
0DD7: 30B5: D0 D1     BNE $3088  Error step
0DD9: 30B7: A0 00     LDY #$00   Index to zero
0DDB: 30B9: 20 4F 31  JSR $314F  Get Data byte (Fast-Mode)
0DDE: 30BC: 91 20     STA ($20),Y Put characters in RAM
0DE0: 30BE: C8        INY        increment the pointer
0DE1: 30BF: D0 F8     BNE $30B9  Still not all the chars
0DE3: 30C1: E6 21     INC $21    Increment pointer's Hi-Byte
0DE5: 30C3: CA        DEX        Decrement the block counter
0DE6: 30C4: D0 EA     BNE $30B0  Further Blocks
0DE8: 30C6: AD 00 DD  LDA $DD00  Get PRA CIA2
0DEB: 30C9: 29 EF     AND #$EF   Mask CLK-Bit
0DED: 30CB: 8D 00 DD  STA $DD00  and back again
0DF0: 30CE: 60        RTS        End of the routine
0DF1: 30CF: A9 0F     LDA #$0F   Put Logical File number 15
0DF3: 30D1: 8D 06 FD  STA $FD06  in $FD06
0DF6: 30D4: 4C 08 30  JMP $3008  Turn onZ-80
0DF9: 30D7: A9 0F     LDA #$0F   Logical file number
0DFB: 30D9: 18        CLC        Erase carry as Flag
0DFC: 30DA: 20 C3 FF  JSR $FFC3  Turn off the channel
0DFF: 30DD: A9 0F     LDA #$0F   Logical file number
0E01: 30DF: 8D 08 FD  STA $FD08  Note logical file number
0E03: 30E2: A2 08     LDX #$08   Device address
0E06: 30E4: A8        TAY        15 as secondary address
0E07: 30E5: 20 BA FF  JSR $FFBA  SETLFS; Set the logical
                                  file parameters
0E0A: 30E8: A9 00     LDA #$00   Turn off the
0E0C: 30EA: 8D 1C 0A  STA $0A1C  floppy's fast mode
0E0F: 30ED: AA        TAX        Set both config. indices
0E10: 30EE: 20 68 FF  JSR $FF68  for SETBNK to zero
0E13: 30F1: A9 04     LDA #$04   Long File name
0E15: 30F3: A2 B8     LDX #$B8   File name's Lo address
0E17: 30F5: A0 31     LDY #$31   File name's Hi address
0E19: 30F7: 20 BD FF  JSR $FFBD  SETNAM; set
                                  Filename parameter
0E1C: 30FA: 20 C0 FF  JSR $FFC0  OPEN the file
0E1F: 30FD: B0 D0     BCS $30CF  error walk, then jump
0E21: 30FF: 20 B7 FF  JSR $FFB7  get Status byte I/O
0E24: 3102: 2A        ROL A      Shift Bit 7 in Carry
```

```
0E25: 3103: B0 CA      BCS $30CF   error walk, then jump
0E27: 3105: 2C 1C 0A   BIT $0A1C   Test the Fast-Serial-Bit
0E2A: 3108: 70 26      BVS $3130   Jump if it is set
0E2C: 310A: A9 0B      LDA #$0B    Logical File number 11
0E2E: 310C: 18         CLC         Erase carry as flag
0E2F: 310D: 20 C3 FF   JSR $FFC3   Close file 11
0E32: 3110: A9 0B      LDA #$0B    Logical file number 11
0E34: 3112: A2 08      LDX #$08    Device # 8
0E36: 3114: A0 08      LDY #$08    Secondary address 8
0E38: 3116: 20 BA FF   JSR $FFBA   SETLFS; Store File data
0E3B: 3119: A9 00      LDA #$00    LFN as not opened
0E3D: 311B: 8D 08 FD   STA $FD08   Erase on $FD08
0E40: 311E: AA         TAX         Both configuration indices
0E41: 311F: 20 68 FF   JSR $FF68   are zero; SETBNK
0E44: 3122: A9 01      LDA #$01    Length of the File name
0E46: 3124: A2 BC      LDX #$BC    Lo-Byte of the Filenamen
0E48: 3126: A0 31      LDY #$31    Hi-Byte of the Filenamen
0E4A: 3128: 20 BD FF   JSR $FFBD   SETNAM; set addr Filename
0E4D: 312B: 20 C0 FF   JSR $FFC0   OPEN 11,8,8,"#"; open file
0E50: 312E: B0 9F      BCS $30CF   error walk
0E52: 3130: 60         RTS         else End of the routine


******************************** Read Track/Sector

0E53: 3131: 20 A4 31   JSR $31A4   Set cmmnd channel to output
0E56: 3134: A0 0D      LDY #$0D    Output 13 character
                                   "U1:8 0 tt ss<CR>"
0E58: 3136: B9 AB 31   LDA $31AB,Y Get chars from table
0E5B: 3139: 20 D2 FF   JSR $FFD2   and output
0E5E: 313C: 88         DEY         Decrement counter,
0E5F: 313D: D0 F7      BNE $3136   jump if ther are more chars
0E61: 313F: 20 CC FF   JSR $FFCC   CLRCH; I/O is normal again
0E64: 3142: 20 89 31   JSR $3189   Open cmmnd channel for read
0E67: 3145: F0 05      BEQ $314C   no error walk
0E69: 3147: A9 0D      LDA #$0D    Set Error
0E6B: 3149: 8D 06 FD   STA $FD06   marker
0E6E: 314C: 4C CC FF   JMP $FFCC   CLRCH; I/O normal again
```

```
********************************* Wait until SDR
                                  (Serial Data Register)
                                  is done, then get data byte

0E71: 314F: 78         SEI        Prevent interruptions
0E72: 3150: AD 00 DD   LDA #$DD00 Get PRA CIA2
0E75: 3153: 49 10      EOR #$10   Negate Clock management
0E77: 3155: 8D 00 DD   STA $DD00  Negate run back
0E7A: 3158: A9 08      LDA #$08   SDR full/empty-Bit
0E7C: 315A: 2C 0D DC   BIT $DC0D  SDR isn't finished yet
0E7F: 315D: F0 FB      BEQ $315A  Wait until timer is low
0E81: 315F: AD 0C DC   LDA $DC0C  Get SDR (Serial Data Reg)
0E84: 3162: 60         RTS        End of the routine
0E85: 3163: AD 0D DC   LDA $DC0D  Erase Interrupt reg in CIA1
0E88: 3166: AD 0D DD   LDA $DD0D  Erase Interrupt reg in CIA2
0E8B: 3169: A9 0F      LDA #$0F   Erase Interrupt register
0E8D: 316B: 8D 19 D0   STA $D019  of the VIC-Chip
0E90: 316E: 68         PLA        Remanufacture
0E91: 316F: 8D 00 FF   STA $FF00  configuration
0E94: 3172: 68         PLA        Remanufacture
0E95: 3173: A8         TAY        Y-Register
0E96: 3174: 68         PLA        Remanufacture
0E97: 3175: AA         TAX        X-Register
0E98: 3176: 68         PLA        Remanufacture accu
0E99: 3177: 40         RTI        End of the
                                   Interrupt-Routine

********************************* Make out of<Accu> 2
                                  ASCII-Codes

0E9A: 3178: D8         CLD        Erase decimal flag
0E9B: 3179: A2 30      LDX #$30   Ten's place is now a "0"
0E9D: 317B: 38         SEC        Set carry flag
                                  for subtraction
0E9E: 317C: E9 0A      SBC #$0A   Subtract ten (test)
0EA0: 317E: 90 03      BCC $3183  Too much subtracted
0EA2: 3180: E8         INX        else increment ten's place
0EA3: 3181: B0 F9      BCS $317C  and do it again
0EA5: 3183: 69 3A      ADC #$3A   Correct error and add
                                  ASCII-Basis
0EA7: 3185: 60         RTS        End of the routine
```

```
******************************** Check if there are errors
                                  in command channel

0EA8: 3186: 20 D7 30   JSR $30D7   error walk in channel 15
0EAB: 3189: A2 0F      LDX #$0F    Open command channel for
0EAD: 318B: 20 C6 FF   JSR $FFC6   reading; CHKIN
0EB0: 318E: B0 F6      BCS $3186   error walk
0EB2: 3190: 20 CF FF   JSR $FFCF   BASIN; get character
0EB5: 3193: C9 30      CMP #$30    Compare accu with "0"
                                    (then OK)
0EB7: 3195: 60         RTS         End of the routine


******************************** Prepare channel 11 (#)
                                  for reading

0EB8: 3196: 20 0A 31   JSR $310A   Error walk in channel 11
0EBB: 3199: A2 0B      LDX #$0B    Set channel 11
0EBD: 319B: 20 C6 FF   JSR $FFC6   to input; CHKIN
0EC0: 319E: B0 F6      BCS $3196   Error walk
0EC2: 31A0: 60         RTS         End of the routine


******************************** Channel 15(command channel)
                                  to output

0EC3: 31A1: 20 D7 30   JSR $30D7   Error walk in channel 15
0EC6: 31A4: A2 0F      LDX #$0F    Channel 15 as output chanel
0EC8: 31A6: 20 C9 FF   JSR $FFC9   Define through
                                    CKOUT-Routine
0ECB: 31A9: B0 F6      BCS $31A1   Error walk
0ECD: 31AB: 60         RTS         End of the routine

0ECE: 31AC: 0D 73 73 20 74 74 20 30     .ss tt 0
0ED6: 31B4: 20 38 3A 31 55 30 4C 00     8:1U0L.
0EDE: 31BC: 23 01 00 00 00 30 55        #....0U

******************************** Will be copied to $FFD0
                                  (8502-Code)

0EE5: ($FFD0) 78         SEI         Prevent interruptions
0EE6: ($FFD1) A9 3E      LDA #$3E    Set config byte to $3E
0EE8: ($FFD3) 8D 00 FF   STA $FF00 RAM and System I/O
```

```
0EEB: ($FFD6) A9 B0      LDA #$B0  Turn on Z-80
0EED: ($FFD8) 8D 05 D5   STA $D505 in MCR
0EF0: ($FFDB) EA         NOP       Wait work
0EF1: ($FFDC) 4C 00 30   JMP $3000 Jump in next routine part
0EF4: ($FFDF) EA         NOP       Buffer


*******************************  Will be copied to $FFE0

0EF5: ($FFE0) F3         DI              Cut offInterruptions
0EF6: ($FFE1) 3E 3E      LD  A,$3E       Set Configuration
0EF8: ($FFE3) 32 00 FF   LD  ($FF00),A byte
0EFB: ($FFE6) 01 05 D5   LD  BC,$D505    Mode-Config.-Register
0EFE: ($FFE9) 3E B1      LD  A,$B1       and turn on 8502
0F00: ($FFEB) ED 79      OUT (C),A       by setting Bit-0
0F02: ($FFED) 00         NOP             Buffer work
0F03: ($FFEE) CF         RST $08         Jump into Z-80 part


******************************* Various tables

0F04:  9E FF BD 58 6F CE/00 0F   Color table
0F0C:  08 07 0B 04 02 0D 0A 0C   adapted for a
0F14:  09 06 01 05 03 0E/00 60   40-character screen
0F1C:  30 18 0C 06 03 00 18 3C
0F24:  66 00 00 00 00 00 00 00
0F2C:  00 00 00 00 7F 00 60 30
0F34:  18 00 00 00 00 00 1C 30
0F3C:  30 60 30 30 1C 00 18 18
0F44:  18 18 18 18 18 00 38 0C
0F4C:  0C 06 0C 0C 38 00 00 1B
0F54:  2A 66 00 00 00 00 00 00
0F5D:  00 00 00 41 7F 00 00 F2
0F64:  5B 39 01 4E 65 37 06 03
0F6C:  1E 07 0B 68 4B 34 17 01
0F74:  44 62 2D 18 12 0B 63 59
0F7C:  31 17 00 0B 59 72 2B 18
0F84:  0F 63 00 4F 2B 05 4C 68
0F8C:  2D 17 16 69 49 25 17 13
0F94:  45 68 29 18 17 07 0C 68
0F9C:  4B 34 13 0F 05 4B 70 31
0FA4:  31 0D 0D 08 08 6C/0D 3F
```

```
0FAC:  7F 3E 7E B0 0B 00 00 01   MMU Register layout
0FB4:  00/00 05 0A 0F 14 04 09   adapted Sector numbers
0FBC:  0E 13 03 08 0D 12 02 07   according to
0FC4:  0C 11 01 06 0B 10 00 05   different sectors.
0FCC:  0A 0F 01 06 0B 10 02 07   In this manner
0FD4:  0C 11 03 08 0D 12 04 09   the layout of the disk will
0FDC:  0E 00 05 0A 0F 02 07 0C   be optimized
0FE4:  11 04 09 0E 01 06 0B 10
0FEC:  03 08 0D 00 05 0A 0F 03
0FF4:  08 0D 01 06 0B 10 04 09
0FFC:  0E 02 07 0C
```

Chapter 10

The CP/M commands

10.1 COPYSYS

This command normally copies the system tracks and CP/M3.SYS to a diskette.

Input format: COPYSYS

Description:

To boot from a CP/M 3.0 diskette, both the system tracks and the CPM+.SYS file must be present. Disks that are not used to boot CP/M do not require either. With the '128, it's quite easy to change the actual format of the COPYSYS command, since the system can be transferred by copying with PIP. If you use the COPYSYS command, a message is displayed telling you that this command is nonfunctional.

10.2 DATE

Displays the date and time, and allows them to be changed.

Input format:

```
DATE
DATE CONTINUOUS
DATE SET
DATE mm/dd/yy hh:mm:ss
```

Description:

This program lets you enter the date and time into your system or to recall that information.

Uses:

If the `DATE` command is entered, the date and time are displayed:

```
Tue 05/06/85 23:49:17.
```

This is a static display. To display the time continously, enter the command `DATE` with the option `C`. The time is displayed until you press any key.

The date and time may be entered in either of two different ways. The `SET` option is used to enter the values for each, one after the other. The other method looks like this:

```
DATE 05/06/85 23:49:17
```

Enter a time that is a few seconds ahead of actual time. Then press the space bar when the times are sychronized to activate the new time..

If your computer does not have a battery-powered clock (the '128 does not), the time must be re-entered each time the computer is turned on. This minor annoyance can be minimized by placing the `DATE SET` command in the `PROFILE.SUB` file.

By entering `DATEC`, you can avoid having to use the `DATE` command followed by the `C` option. The source file for the `DATE` program is saved on the system diskette. Observing its operation may teach you a lot.

10.3 DEVICE

Displays and alters the devices used to access the peripherals.

Input format:

```
DEVICE NAMES
DEVICE VALUES
DEVICE LST:=xxxxxx[NOXON,1200]
DEVICE CONOUT:=xxx,xxx
DEVICE CON:[PAGES]
DEVICE CON:[COLUMNS=nn, LINES=mm]
```

Description:

This program is used to display and assign input and output devices to the operating system. The names of the three logical devices are: CON:, LST:, and AUX:. A logical device can also be set to several peripherals. For instance, data may be sent to a printer and the monitor at the same time. DEVICE also controls the # rows/columns displayed on the monitor.

Uses:

The names of the output devices are predetermined by the Commodore CP/M system. If DEVICE is entered with the NAMES option, a list with the names and baud rates of the individual is displayed. If DEVICE VALUES is entered, the following is displayed:

Current Assignments:

```
CONIN:   = KEYS
CONOUT:  = 40 COL   (or 80 COL)
AUXIN:   = Null device
AUXOUT:  = Null device
LST:     = PRT1
```

CONIN: and CONOUT: refer to console input (or keyboard input), and console output (or keyboard output.) CON: alone refers to both input and output. LST: stands for LIST DEVICE and refers to the printer. Using the PAGE option, you can find out how many rows and columns are presently being displayed by the monitor.

If a specific baud rate is entered in the format [*nnn*], the data-exchange with the particular peripheral is executed at this speed. The command DEVICE displays DEVICE NAMES and VALUES together.

```
A>DEVICE


Physical Devices:
I=Input, O=Output, S=Serial, X=Xon-Xoff
KEYS   NONE  I      80COL  NONE  O      40COL  NONE  O
PRT1   NONE  O      PRT2   NONE  O      6551   9600  IOSX
RS232  300   IOSX

Current Assignments:
CONIN:  = KEYS
CONOUT: = Null Device
AUXIN:  = Null Device
LST:    = PRT1

Enter new assignment or hit RETURN
```

Note: The command `DEVICE` replaces the `STAT DEV`: command in CP/M 3.0. (The `STAT` command of CP/M 2.2 was divided, since it was too complex).

10.4 DIR

Displays specified file names of the directory.

Input format:

Resident command: `DIR`
`DIR A:`
`DIR DATEI.xxx`
`DIR AB*.*`

Transient command: DIR[*option*]
DIR DATEI.xxx[*option*]
DIR AB*.*[*option*]

Description:

`DIR` disaplays the filenames on a diskette or hard disk drive. Wild-card characters may be used to filter the filenames. The wild card characters are `*` and `?`. If no option is chosen, all non-system files will be marked for the corresponding user area.

The `DIR` transient command is much more versatile. It displays files with date stamps, can alphabetize them, etc. An explanation of the various options, which must be entered in brackets, follows.

If the system files are in the directory, the following message will appear:

```
SYSTEM FILE(S) EXIST
```

Options:

Option	Function
ATT	display user-defined file attributes
DATE	display data with time and date
DIR	display non-system files
DRIVE=ALL	display files in all drives
DRIVE=A	display files in drive A
EXCLUDE	display all files except the one specified
FF	send form feed to printer
FULL	display files with complete description
LENGTH=n	send form feed after n lines
MESSAGE	scrolling display of disk drives/USER areas
NOPAGE	scrolling display
RO	display read-only files
RW	display read/write files
SIZE	display size of each file
SYS	display only system files
USER=ALL	display files of all USER areas
USER=5	display files of the USER area that was specified
USER=(3,5)	display files of the USER areas that were specified

10.5 DIRSYS

This command, lists files specified as SYSTEM files.

Input format:

```
DIRSYS
DIRSYS B:
DIRSYS Filename.xxx
DIRSYS AB?*.*
```

Description

With the DIRSYS command, all SYSTEM files can be diplayed. This may be accomplished using the DIR with options, but DIRSYS is much faster, since it is a Resident command. The command can be abbreviated as DIRS.

The DIRSYS command also tells you whether any "normal" files exist (CP/M refers to them as *non-system files*). If there are no system files, this message is displayed:

```
No File
```

10.6 DUMP

Displays non-text files in hexadecimal and ASCII format.

Input format: `DUMP`
`DUMP` *Filename*.xxx

Description:

`DUMP` displays the contents of a file in both hexadecimal and ASCII format.

To display ASCII only text files you can use the `TYPE` command. But `COM`, `REL`, or `OVR` files, for example should be examined using `DUMP`.

The lefthand columns contain the relative address of the file contents. The middle columns contain the hexidecimal contents. The righthand columns contain the corresponding ASCII characters. A character whose value cannot be displayed is indicated by a period (.). You can also send the display to the printer by pressing <CONTROL> P.

10.7 ED

The CP/M editor.

Input format: ED*<filename>* (.*<file type>*)

Description:

The built-in editor may be practical for very short texts, but it has a bad operational reputation—for good reason. The editor is extremely complicated and is difficult to operate, even for experienced users.

When the file name is entered, ED checks if it presently exists. If it does, the file is loaded into the ED buffer and a backup file is created. If the file does not presently exist, the following message is displayed:

```
Enter Input file
```

After you enter the file name, it displays:

```
Enter Output file
```

To exit the editor, even when saving the data, simply enter the command E.

Here's a list of all of ED's commands:

Command	Function
*n*A	append *n* lines from original file to memory buffer
0A	append file until buffer is one half full
#A	append file until buffer is full (or end of file)
B, -B	move cursor position to the beginning (B) or bottom (-B) of buffer

*n*C, -*n*C	move cursor position *n* characters forward (C) or back (-C) through buffer
*n*D, -*n*D	delete *n* characters before (-D) or from (D) the cursor position
E	save new file, return to CP/M
F*string* <CONTROL Z>	find character string
H	save new file, re-edit, use new file as original file
I<RETURN>	enter insert mode
I*string*<CONTROL> Z	insert string at cursor position
J*search_str*<CONTROL> Z *ins_str*<CONTROL>Z*del_to_str*	switch strings
*n*K, -*n*K	delete *n* lines from the cursor position
*n*L, -*n*L, 0L	move cursor position *n* lines
*n*Mcommands	execute commands *n* times
n, -*n*	move cursor position *n* lines and display that line
n:	move to line *n*
:*n*command	execute command through line *n*
n string<CONTROL> Z	extended find string
O	return to original file

*n*P, -*n*P	move cursor position 23 lines forward and display 23 lines at console
Q	abandon new file, return to CP/M-86
R<CONTROL> Z	read X$$$$$$$.LIB file into buffer
R*filename*<CONTROL> Z	read filename into buffer
S*del. string*<CONTROL>Z	insert substitute string
*n*T, -*n*T, 0T	type *n* lines
U, -U	upper-case translation
V, -V	line numbering on/off
0V	display free buffer space
*n*W	write *n* lines to new file
0W	write until buffer is half empty
*n*X	write or append *n* lines to X$$$$$$$.LIB
*n*X*filename*<CONTROL> Z	write *n* lines to filename; append if previous X command applied to same file
0X<CONTROL> Z	delete file X$$$$$$$.LIB
0X*filename*<CONTROL> Z	delete filename
*n*Z	wait *n* seconds

Note: the cursor position points to the character currently being referenced in the edit buffer. Use a <CONTROL> Z to separate multiple commands on the same line.

10.8 ERA(SE)

Resident command to erase one, several, or all files on a diskette.

Input format:

Resident command: `ERASE`
`ERASE` *Filename*`.xxx`
`ERASE AB?*.*`

Transient command: `ERASE` *Filename*`.xxx [CONFIRM]`

Description:

The `ERASE` command will erase a specified file, if that file is not a read-only file, or write-protected. You can erase a file only within the same `USER` area. If you specify a filename containing `*` or `?`, you are asked to confirm the command by entering `Y` or `N`.

Uses:

`ERASE` may be abbreviated to `ERA`. The option `CONFIRM` can be abbreviated to `C`.

10.9 FORMAT

Formats a floppy diskette.

Input format: FORMAT

Description:

All diskettes used with the C-128 must be formatted properly. All previous data on a diskette is lost during formatting. FORMAT is not a standard CP/M program.

Uses:

After a diskette is FORMATed, you are asked the question format another disk? This allows you to format several diskettes, one after the other.

Note: Several diskette formats are possible with the Commodore 128. Because of this, when you format, you will be asked whether you want to format the diskette as single-sided or double-sided. With the FORMAT command, diskettes may only be formatted in drive A.

10.10 GENCOM

Generates a special version of CP/M 3.0.

Input format: `GENCOM`

Description:

Is used by programmers to adapt a CP/M version, or to integrate additional program-routines in CP/M.

10.11 GET

Gets data from a file instead of the keyboard.

Input format:

```
GET CONSOLE INPUT FROM FILE Filename.xxx
GET CONSOLE INPUT FROM CONSOLE
GET FILE Filename.xxx[NOECHO]
```

Description:

The GET command enables you to read data from a particular file instead of the keyboard.

Uses:

In the first example, CP/M retrieves commands from a file named *Filename*.xxx. If there are no more commands in the file, CP/M reverts to keyboard input.

The the second example, CP/M retrieves commands from the keyboard.

In the third example, CP/M retrieves commands from the keyboard.The (NOECHO) option ispecifies that the commands are not displayed on the screen.

10.12 HELP

Provides information about the individual CP/M commands, with examples.

Input format:

```
HELP
HELP Keyword
HELP Keyword (abbreviation)
HELP Keyword[option]
HELP (abbreviated) Keyword
HELP [option]
```

Description:

The `HELP.COM` command displays information about the CP/M commands and programs. `HELP` cannot be used while a program is running. `HELP [EXTRACT]` creates a `HELP.DAT` file that can be edited with an editor.

Uses:

The `HELP` command displays information based on keyword. The keyword may be abbreviated to two characters. If the information is longer than 23 lines, the display stops when the screen is filled. To continue, simply press the space bar. If <CONTROL> P is activated beforehand, all information is sent to the printer.

The available keywords are:

C128_CP/M	COMMANDS	CNTRLCHARS	COPYSYS	DATE	DEVICE
DIR	DUMP	ED	ERASE	FILESPEC	GENCOM
GET	HELP	HEXCOM	INITDIR	KEYFIG	LIB
LINK	MAC	PATCH	PIP(COPY)	PUT	RENAME
RMAC	SAVE	SET	SETDEF	SHOW	SID
SUBMIT	TYPE	USER	XREF		

10.13 HEXCOM (Additional Utilities)

Creates a COM file that can be executed.

Input format: HEXCOM<*Filename*>
HEXCOM

Description:

This command converts a HEX file to a COM file. You do not have to specify the file extension, since HEXCOM adds .HEX to the filename.

Don't use HEXCOM to change RMAC.HEX files into COM files. .HEX files created by RMAC (the relocatable code-producing assembler),must be processed by the LINK command.

10.14 INITDIR

Prepares a diskette's directory to accept a time and date stamp.

Input format: `INITDIR B:`

Description:

CP/M 3.0 lets you mark files with a time and date stamp. This information is stored in a separate part of the directory. Because of this, the directory must be prepared by using INITDIR. The nature of the file types may be controlled with the command SET.

Uses:

It is best to use INITDIR on a new diskette, since timestamps require diskette space. If you are using INITDIR on a diskette containing data, make a backup of that diskette first. If INITDIR were interrupted, the data on that diskette may be lost.

10.15 KEYFIG

KEYFIG enables you to reassign the values of each key, and lets you define the function keys.

Input format: KEYFIG

Description:

The KEYFIG command is menu-oriented. KEYFIG provides you with HELP screens. The command lets you assign any ASCII value to any key, using <SHIFT> or <CTRL>. It also lets you define colors, and lets you assign special functions to keys (such as rebooting of the system, etc.). Finally, KEYFIG allows you to define function keys such as the HELP key. Thus this command proves to be very helpful.

10.16 `LIB` (Additional Utilities)

Produces and changes a "library" of subprograms.

Input format: LIB *Filename*.XXX[OPTIONS]

Description:

Many compilers and the assemblers RMAC and MACRO-80 use the method of subprograms, which usually have the extension REL or IRL. Listing of important subprograms in a library is done by using LIB.

10.17 LINK (Additional Utilities)

Produces a file which can be executed from subprogram modules.

Input format: LINK *Filename,Filename2,Filename3,...*[OPTIONS]

Description:

Many compilers and the assemblers RMAC and MACRO-80 create REL or IRL programs. LINK lets you combine these files into a single COM file.

10.18 MAC (Additional Utilities)

A macroassembler in 8080-mnemonic and restricted for Z-80 and 6502-mnemonic.

Input format: `MAC` *Filename*
`MAC` *Filename* `$OPTIONS`

Description:

The macroassembler creates three files. The extension of the source program is `ASM`. The extension of the library is `LIB`. The assembled program code (object code) has the extension `HEX`, the symbol schedule with the extension `SYM`, and the printable listing the extension `PRN`. Options are marked with a dollar sign (`$`) instead of the usual brackets.

More detailed information about the `MAC` assembler is found in Chapter 7.

10.19 PATCH

Installs changes in CP/M 3.0 or other programs

Input format: `PATCH` *Filename*
`PATCH` *Filename n*

Description:

You can use the `PATCH` command to make program changes in existing CP/M transient programs. This process is known as patching. `PATCH` automatically enters the changes in the specific program, and if several patches are made, they are identified with reference numbers (*n*). The reference numbers start with 1.

10.20 PIP

Copies files and transfers files between peripherals.

Input format:

```
PIP
PIP Destination file=Source file [options]
PIP B:=Filename.XXX
COMBFILE.txt=TEXT1.TXT,TEXT2.TXT...
PIP AB1?*.*=AB2?*.*[option]
```

Description:

PIP is easily the most powerful command in CP/M. It lets you copy files, not only from one diskette to another, but also between various user areas. It can combine several files into one, protect files, convert text to uppercase, renumber lines, and change the 8th bit to zero. Chapter 6 contains more detailed information on PIP.

Uses:

PIP can be used with or without options. The PIP prompt is an asterisk is displayed (*). The *Destination file* as an exact duplicate of the *Source file*, unless changed by an option. The brackets must immediately follow the filename without spaces. If several versions of a file are to be copied, or if there are unknown characters in the filename, you may use ? for unknown characters or * for all characters. The default disk drive is the logged drive . Here are some examples:

PIP B:=*Filename*.xxx[V]

This particular command copies the file *Filename*.XXX from drive A to drive B, and verifies that copy.

PIP B:=*Filename*.*[V]

This command copies a series of files with the name *Filename*, regardless of extension, from drive A to B.

`PIP B=*.*[V]`

This copies all files of a diskette to the other drive. The copy is also verified.

`PIP FILENEW.XXX=FILEOLD.XXX`

This command reproduces the file `FILEOLD` as `FILENEW` on the same diskette. Both files will then exist on that diskette.

`PIP COMBFILE.TXT=TEXT1.TXT,TEXT2.TXT,...`

All specified files will be copied into one file, `COMB.TXT`.

`PIP B:[G] =TEXT.TXT[G5]`

The command copies `TEXT.TXT` to drive B, form drive `A`, user area 5.

<u>Options:</u>

A Archive function. Copies only those files that were created or changed since the latest archive update. The time and date stamp function must be set.

C Confirm. CP/M will check after each file to confirm that it may be copied.

Dn Erase after n columns. `PIP` will erase all characters positioned after n columns in the file. Used for text files only.

E Echo text on the monitor. The content of the files being copied are displayed on the screen. Not to be used with the parameter `N`. Used for text files only.

F Form feed. Some printers require a <CTRL> L to feed the next page. If this is not the case, use `F` to erase them.

Gn Get a file from user area n. This option must be positioned directly after the first filename and should be the only thing written there. For example:

```
PIP B:[G5]=TEXT.TXT.TXT[G1]
```

will copy the file `TEXT.TXT` from `USER` area 1 to `USER` area 5.

H Transfer hexadecimal data. This option should always be entered if you want to copy `HEX` files. `PIP` will then check the file content for correct INTEL format.

I Ignore the end-of-file marker in `HEX` files. Enter this option for every file except the last one. Along with the option `I`, the option `H` is entered by `PIP`. For the last file use the parameter `H`:

`PIP` *Filename*`.HEX=PROG1.HEX[I],PROG2.HEX[H]`

K Suppress the display of filenames during copying.

L Change all capital letters to lowercase. Use this option only for text files, and be sure to use the parameter `Z` for WordStar files.

N Numbers the lines of a file continuously. The numbers start with 1 in the first line, and increase by 1 for each line. The numbers can have a maximum of 6 digits. Unused digits will appear as spaces. The numbers will be followed by a colon and a space. Do not use with the options `E` or `N`. Choose parameter `Z` for WordStar files.

N2 Numbers the lines for a BASIC program.

O Transfer of object-files. Used to transfer non-text and non-`COM` files. Do not use for text files.

Pn Sets page length. Default is 60 lines per page. Enter the `F` option to erase any <CTRL> L (form feed) markers that may exist. Use only with text files.

Qxxxx<CTRL>Z

Quit copying after this character string. PIP will copy a file up to and including the specified character string. Use the command in command lines so that the string will not be changed to capital letters. Use only for text files:

```
PIP
CON:=TEXT.TXT[Hamlet]
```

If command is one line, the entry appears in capital letters.

R Copy system files. These files are not listed by DIR, and PIP does not usually copy them. R will cancel these restrictions.

Sxxxx<CTRL>Z

Start at this character string. PIP will begin copying at this character string. Be sure to write the command in two lines, otherwise the text is changed to all capital letters. Use only with text files.

Tn Set tab. Normally CP/M operates with an 8-space tab. This is not the case for hardcopies, and thus the tab must be defined. **n** specifies the number of spaces the tab is set. Use with text files only.

U Capitalize. Changes all lower case characters to upper case. Use only with text files. When used with WordStar, be sure to use the option Z.

V Verify. This parameter verifies files copied by PIP. It ensures that the new file is identical to the old one.

W Write over read-only files. These files may normally be read, but not changed or erased. The W option causes these files to be erased without recall.

Z Erase the 8th bit. ASCII uses only seven bits, and the 8th bit is utilized by many applications programs for various functions. The Z option is not necessary when copying ASCII data, such as COM: or LST:.

10.21 PUT

Redirects data intended for the monitor to printer or a file.

Input format:

```
PUT CONSOLE OUTPUT TO FILE Filename.xxx[option]
PUT PRINTER OUTPUT TO FILE Filename.xxx[option]
PUT CONSOLE OUTPUT TO CONSOLE
PUT PRINTER OUTPUT TO PRINTER
```

Description:

Normally CP/M sends data to the monitor. The `PUT` command allows you to write the data to a file or the printer.

Uses:

The first examples direct CP/M to open a file and write all output intended for the screen or printer to that file. Once the operation is ended, CP/M will return to its normal mode. The last two examples terminate the `PUT` command. For example, these could be used if you had a `SUBMIT` file using the `PUT` command, and should subsequently return to normal mode.

The display of the data on the monitor can be terminated with the command `ECHO`. The option `FILTER` changes all control characters into printable form.

The option `SYSTEM` causes the commands to be saved along with the data in the new file.

10.22 REN(AME)

Renames an existing file.

Input format:

```
RENAME
RENAME Filename2.xxx=Filename1.xxx
RENAME AB?*2=AB?*1
```

Description:

The command RENAME does not change the data, only the filename. The content of the file will remain intact.

Uses:

If the file is not on the default drive A, you may specify the drive along with the RENAME command. Should the RENAME command be entered without options, the program asks which drive to use.

If, during the RENAME operation, the old file is to be overwritten, then the program asks you whether that old file should be erased. If you answer no, the RENAME operation is halted.

10.23 RMAC (Additional Utilities)

Macroassembler for programming in assembly language. Creates the relocatable object code, which must be processed by `LINK`.

Input format: `RMAC` *Filename*
`RMAC` *Filename* `$` *options*

Description:

The `RMAC` macroassembly produces three files. The source program is listed with the extension `ASM`, and the library with the extension `LIB`. The assembled program code is listed with the extension `REL`, the symbol schedule with `SYM` and the printable listing with `PRN`. The command `LINK` creates a file from the `REL` file which can be executed.

Uses:

Instead of the usual brackets, dollar signs (`$`) are used to indicate options. The option must be preceded by a space.

10.24 SAVE

Saves the data (program) currently in memory onto a diskette.

Input format: `SAVE`

Description:

The `SAVE` command lets you create a file on diskette. To use this command, you enter `SAVE` <RETURN>. SAVE then makes preaparation so that CP/M will be able to save the subsequent program.

Uses:

`SAVE` is automatically placed at the upper end of the memory, and returns control to CP/M after it is located there. Next enter the program name of the program to be saved. After it is loaded, `SAVE` will regain control and you are asked for the filename and the starting and ending addresses.

10.25 SET

Sets the file attributes, enables the input of a password, assigns disk labels, and chooses the format of the time and date stamps.

Input format:

SET *Filename*.xxx[*option*]
SET AB?*.*[*option*]
SET B:[*option*]
SET[*option*]

Description:

The SET program serves several purposes. Its most important tasks are: setting the archive mode and declaring diskettes or drives as read-only or write-only.

Each diskette can be assigned its own name, and passwords can be assigned to the whole diskette and/or individual files. The diskette labels may be displayed using SHOW.

Also, such files may be equipped with time and date stamps.

SET *filename*.COM [SYS] allows the file to be accessed from any user area.

For more detailed information, see Chapter 5.

10.26 SETDEF

Displays and defines the order of disk drive search and turns the screen output on or off.

Input format:

```
SETDEF
SETDEF B:
SETDEF[option]
```

Description:

Normally, transient programs are started by typing the name and pressing <RETURN>. If the program is to be loaded from a different drive, a drive must be specified along with the name.

For instance, if you always work on drive B and your CP/M system files are on drive A, you can tell CP/M on to search drive B first. This is known as specifying a search order. This way you can tell CP/M to seach first on drive A, then on drive C:, and only then on the default drive.

10.27 SHOW

Displays the options of a diskette.

Input format: `SHOW`[*option*]
`SHOW B:`[*option*]

Description:

`SHOW` displays the technical data of a diskette directory. The disk's free space, the number of entries in the directory, the number of active `USER` areas, and the chosen `USER` area number, the total diskette capacity, block size, sector size, and number of sectors per track, and the name of a diskette are displayed.

`SHOW` is actually a useful addition to `DIR`. With `SHOW` you can also find out if the diskette and/or individual files are protected by passwords.

Options are:

```
SPACE
LABEL
USERS
DIR
DRIVE
```

10.28 SID (Symbolic Interactive Debugger)

A debugging program to load, change, and test assembler programs.

Input format:

```
SID
SID Filename.xxx
SID Filename.xxx TEXT.SYM
```

Description:

SID lets you load COM and HEX files into memory, and then view and edit them. The program may be run with enhanced control if a SYM file is loaded. SID can also change executable programs into INTEL 8080 mnemonics.

Unfortunately this program is available only on the Additional Utilities diskette. SID is a further development of the DDT program in CP/M 2.2.

10.29 `SUBMIT`

Enables command input from a file, instead of the keyboard

Input format: `SUBMIT` *filename, parameter 1,parm 2...,parm n*

Description:

A series of commands usually entered through the keyboard can also be written to a `SUBMIT` file, and then be executed automatically. When the file of commands is completed, control is returned to CP/M.

With each power-up, CP/M checks a file called `PROFILE.SUB` and automatically executes any commands in that file (if the file is found).

Uses:

To write a `SUBMIT` file with your text program, simply write the desired commands each on a line. The extension for this file must be `SUB`—otherwise it not recognized by `SUBMIT`.

10.30 USER

Changes the current user area.

Input format: USER
USER n

Description:

Each diskette may be divided into 16 different user areas. Thus you can have separate user areas for various jobs, in which the necessary files and programs are stored. System files, located in the user level 0, may be read from any user area.

Uses:

The current user area is displayed in the CP/M prompt (1B>), and may be changed with the USER command. If you do not specify the new area, the program will ask you for it. The program SHOW will display the active user areas.

10.31 XREF (Additional Utilities)

Creates a cross-reference listing for assembler programs.

Input format: XREF *Filename*
XREF *Filename* $P

Description:

The MAC and RMAC assemblers produce an alphabetical list of all symbols used and their values in a program. XREF is more practical, since in addition to the symbols it displays the program lines those symbols are found in. XREF requires SYM files and PRN files. XREF produces an assembler list called *<Filename>*.XRF (similar to *<Filename>*.PRN) and includes a detailed listing of all symbols present, and the line numbers at which those symbols appear in the program.

Appendices

Appendix A: ASCII and Number Conversion Table

Decimal	Hexa-decimal	Binary	ASCII
0	00	000 0000	NUL
1	01	000 0001	SOH
2	02	000 0010	STX
3	03	000 0011	ETX
4	04	000 0100	EOT
5	05	000 0101	ENQ
6	06	000 0110	ACU
7	07	000 0111	BEL
8	08	000 1000	ES
9	09	000 1001	HT
10	0A	000 1010	LF
11	0B	000 1011	VT
12	0C	000 1100	FF
13	0D	000 1101	CR
14	0E	000 1110	SO
15	0F	000 1111	SI
16	10	001 0000	DLE
17	11	001 0001	DC1
18	12	001 0010	DC2
19	13	001 0011	DC3
20	14	001 0100	DC4
21	15	001 0101	AAK
22	16	001 0110	SYU
23	17	001 0111	ETB
24	18	001 1000	CAN

Decimal	Hexa-decimal	Binary	ASCII
25	19	001 1001	EM
26	1A	001 1010	SUB
27	1B	001 1011	ESC
28	1C	001 1100	FS
29	1D	001 1101	GS
30	1E	001 1110	RS
31	1F	001 1111	VS
32	20	010 0000	SP
33	21	010 0001	!
34	22	010 0010	"
35	23	010 0011	#
36	24	010 0100	$
37	25	010 0101	%
38	26	010 0110	&
39	27	010 0111	'
40	28	010 1000	(
41	29	010 1001	)
42	2A	010 1010	*
43	2B	010 1011	+
44	2C	010 1100	,
45	2D	010 1101	-
46	2E	010 1110	.
47	2F	010 1111	/
48	30	011 0000	0
49	31	011 0001	1
50	32	011 0010	2
51	33	011 0011	3

Decimal	Hexa-decimal	Binary	ASCII
52	34	011 0100	4
53	35	011 0101	5
54	36	011 0110	6
55	37	011 0111	7
56	38	011 1000	8
57	39	011 1001	9
58	3A	011 1010	:
59	3B	011 1011	;
60	3C	011 1100	<
61	3D	011 1101	=
62	3E	011 1110	>
63	3F	011 1111	?
64	40	100 0000	@
65	41	100 0001	A
66	42	100 0010	B
67	43	100 0011	C
68	44	100 0100	D
69	45	100 0101	E
70	46	100 0110	F
71	47	100 0111	G
72	48	100 1000	H
73	49	100 1001	I
74	4A	100 1010	J
75	4B	100 1011	K
76	4C	100 1100	L
77	4D	100 1101	M
78	4E	100 1110	N

Decimal	Hexa-decimal	Binary	ASCII
79	4F	100 1111	O
80	50	101 0000	P
81	51	101 0001	Q
82	52	101 0010	R
83	53	101 0011	S
84	54	101 0100	T
85	55	101 0101	U
86	56	101 0110	V
87	57	101 0111	W
88	58	101 1000	X
89	59	101 1001	Y
90	5A	101 1010	Z
91	5B	101 1011	[
92	5C	101 1100	\
93	5D	101 1101	]
94	5E	101 1110	^
95	5F	101 1111	_
96	60	110 0000	
97	61	110 0001	a
98	62	110 0010	b
99	63	110 0011	c
100	64	110 0100	d
101	65	110 1101	e
102	66	110 0110	f
103	67	110 0111	g
104	68	110 1000	h
105	69	110 1001	i

Decimal	Hexa-decimal	Binary	ASCII
106	6A	110 1010	j
107	6B	110 1011	k
108	6C	110 1100	l
109	6D	110 1101	m
110	6E	110 1110	n
111	6F	110 1111	o
112	70	111 0000	p
113	71	111 0001	q
114	72	111 0010	r
115	73	111 0011	s
116	74	111 0100	t
117	75	111 0101	u
118	76	111 0110	v
119	77	111 0111	w
120	78	111 1000	x
121	79	111 1001	y
122	7A	111 1010	z
123	7B	111 1011	{
124	7C	111 1100	:
125	7D	111 1101	}
126	7E	111 1110	`
127	7F	111 1111	DEL

Appendix B: CP/M Control Codes

Control Character	Function
<CONTROL> A	moves cursor one character to the left
<CONTROL> B	moves cursor from beginning to end of command line and back without affecting command
<CONTROL> C	stops executing program when entered at the system prompt or after <CONTROL> S
<CONTROL> E	forces a physical carriage return without sending command to CP/M
<CONTROL> F	moves cursor one character to the right
<CONTROL> G	deletes character at current cursor position if in the middle of a line
<CONTROL> I	same as the TAB key
<CONTROL> H	delete character to the left of cursor
<CONTROL> J	moves cursor to the left of the command line and sends command to CP/M 3. Line feed, has same effect as carriage return
<CONTROL> K	deletes character at cursor and all characters to the right
<CONTROL> M	same as carriage return
<CONTROL> P	echoes console output to the list device
<CONTROL> Q	restarts screen scrolling after a <CONTROL> S
<CONTROL> R	retypes the characters to the left of the cursor on a new line; updates the command line buffer
<CONTROL> S	stops screen scrolling

<CONTROL> U	updates the command line buffer to contain the characters to the left of the cursor; deletes current line.
<CONTROL> W	recalls previous command line if current line is empty; otherwise moves cursor to end of line. <CONTROL> J,-M,-R,-U and <RETURN> update the command line buffer for recall with <CONTROL> W.
<CONTROL> X	deletes all characters to the left of the cursor.

Appendix C: `PIP` Command

Options	Function
A	Archive function. Copies only those files that were created or changed since the latest archive update. The time and date stamp function must be set
C	Confirm. CP/M will check after each file to confirm that it may be copied
D*n*	Erase after *n* columns. `PIP` will erase all characters positioned after n columns in the file. Used for text files only
E	Echo text on the monitor. The content of the files being copied are displayed on the screen. Not to be used with the parameter `N`. Used for text files only
F	Form feed. Some printers require a <CTRL> L to feed the next page. If this is not the case, use `F` to erase them
G*n*	Get a file from user area *n*. This option must be positioned directly after the first filename and should be the only thing written there. For example: `PIP B:[G5]=TEXT.TXT.TXT[G1]` will copy the file `TEXT.TXT` from `USER` area 1 to `USER` area 5
H	Transfer hexadecimal data. This option should always be entered if you want to copy `HEX` files. `PIP` will then check the file content for correct INTEL format
I	Ignore the end-of-file marker in `HEX` files. Enter this option for every file except the last one. Along with the option `I`, the option `H` is entered by `PIP`. For the last file use the parameter `H`: `PIP` *Filename*`.HEX=PROG1.HEX[I],PROG2.HEX[H]`

K	Suppress the display of filenames during copying
L	Change all capital letters to lowercase. Use this option only for text files, and be sure to use the parameter `Z` for WordStar files
N	Numbers the lines of a file continuously. The numbers start with 1 in the first line, and increase by 1 for each line. The numbers can have a maximum of 6 digits. Unused digits will appear as spaces. The numbers will be followed by a colon and a space. Do not use with the options `E` or `N`. Choose parameter `Z` for WordStar files
N2	Numbers the lines for a BASIC program
O	Transfer of object-files. Used to transfer non-text and non-`COM` files. Do not use for text files
P*n*	Sets page length. Default is 60 lines per page. Enter the `F` option to erase any <CTRL> L (form feed) markers that may exist. Use only with text files

Qxxxx<CTRL>Z

Quit copying after this character string. `PIP` will copy a file up to and including the specified character string. Use the command in command lines so that the string will not be changed to capital letters. Use only for text files:

```
PIP
CON:=TEXT.TXT[Hamlet]
```

If command is one line, the entry appears in capital letters

R	Copy system files. These files are not listed by `DIR`, and `PIP` does not usually copy them. `R` will cancel these restrictions

Sxxxx<CTRL>Z

Start at this character string. `PIP` will begin copying at this character string. Be sure to write the command in two lines, otherwise the text is changed to all capital letters. Use only with text files

`T`*n*	Set tab. Normally CP/M operates with an 8-space tab. This is not the case for hardcopies, and thus the tab must be defined. *n* specifies the number of spaces the tab is set. Use with text files only
`U`	Capitalize. Changes all lower case characters to upper case. Use only with text files. When used with WordStar, be sure to use the option `Z`
`V`	Verify. This parameter verifies files copied by `PIP`. It ensures that the new file is identical to the old one
`W`	Write over read-only files. These files may normally be read, but not changed or erased. The `W` option causes these files to be erased without recall
`Z`	Erase the 8th bit. ASCII uses only seven bits, and the 8th bit is utilized by many applications programs for various functions. The `Z` option is not necessary when copying ASCII data, such as `COM`: or `LST`:

Appendix D: SET Command

Option	Attributes
RO	sets the file attribute to Read-Only
RW	sets the file attribute to Read-Write
SYS	sets the file attribute to SYS; means that the file is available from any USER area
DIR	sets the file attribute to DIR
ARCHIVE=OFF	means file has not been backed up (archived)
ARCHIVE=ON	means that the file has been backed up (archived). The Archive attribute can be turned on by SET or by PIP when copying a group of files with the PIP [A] option. SHOW and DIR display the Archive option
F1=ON|OFF	turns on or off the user-definable file attribute F1
F2=ON|OFF	turns on or off the user-definable file attribute F2
F3=ON|OFF	turns on or off the user-definable file attribute F3
F4=ON|OFF	turns on or off the user-definable file attribute F4
CREATE=ON	turns on CREATE time stamps on the disk in the default or specified drive. To record the creation time of a file, the CREATE option must be turned on before the file is created
ACCESS=ON	turns on ACCESS time stamps on the disk in the default or specified drive. ACCESS and CREATE options are mutually exclusive; only one can be in effect at a time. If you turn on the ACCESS time stamp on a disk that previously had CREATE time stamp, the CREATE time stamp is automatically turned off

UPDATE=ON	turns on UPDATE time stamps on the disk in the default or specified drive. UPDATE time stamps record the time the file was last modified
PROTECT=ON	turns on password protection for all the files on the disk. You must turn on password protection before you can assign passwords to files
PROTECT=OFF	Disables password protection for the files on your disk
PROTECT=READ	The password is required for reading, copying writing, deleting or renaming the file
PROTECT=WRITE	The password is required for writing, deleting or renaming the file. You do not need a password to read the file
PROTECT=DELETE	The password is only required for deleting or renaming the file. You do not need a password to read or modify the file
PROTECT=NONE	No password exists for the file. If a password password exists, this modifier can be used to delete the password

Appendix E: 8080 Instruction Set

This is a summary of the 8080 instruction set, listed alphabetically, to assist you when programming with the Additional Utilities diskette.

For a complete listing and explanation of 8080 mnemonics, we suggest you purchase one of the many excellent 8080/Z-80 assembly language reference books.

Letters A,B,C,D,E,H,I,L,L,IX,IY, R, and SP are the standard register names. The symbols BC, DE, and HL are used for the register pairs. The symbol nn signifies an 8-bit constant, and the symbol nnnn signifies a 16-bit constant.

Hex		Mnemonic		Notes
CE	nn	ACI	nn	Add nn to acculaulator with carry
8F-8E		ADC	A-M	Add memory byte pointer to by register to accumulator with carry
87-86		ADD	A-M	Add register given to accumulator without carry
C6	nn	ADI	nn	Add the immediate byte to the accumulator
A7-6		ANA	A-M	Logical "and" reg with A, as above
E6	nn	ANI	nn	Perform logical AND with accumulator & nn

CD	nnnn	CALL	nnnn	Unconditional subroutine call to address nnnn
DC	nnnn	CC	nnnn	Conditional subroutine call to address nnnn, carry flag set
FC	nnnn	CM	nnnn	Conditional subroutine call to address nnnn, sign flag set
2F		CMA		Perform one's complement on acculculator
3F		CMC		Complement carry flag
BF-BE		CMP	A-M	Complare byte pointed to by register with accumulator
D4	nnnn	CNC	nnnn	Conditional subroutine call Carry flag set
C4	nnnn	CNZ	nnnn	Conditional subroutine call Zero flag reset
F4	nnnn	CP	nnnn	Conditional subroutine call Sign flag set
EC	nnnn	CPE	nnnn	Conditional subroutine call Parity flag set
FE	nn	CPI	nn	Compare nn to acculumator
E4	nnnn	CPO	nnnn	Conditional subroutine call Parity flag reset

CC	nnnn	CZ	nnnn	Conditional subroutine call Zero flag set
27		DAA		Decimal adjust accumulator
09-39		DAD	B-SP	Add specified double register
3D-35		DCR	A-M	Decrement register
0B-3B		DCX	B-SP	Decrement double register
F3		DI		Disable the interrupt system
FB		EI		Enable the interrupt system
76		HLT		Halt the 8080 processor
DB	nn	IN	nn	Load register A with data from port e8
3C-34		INR	A-M	Single precision increment register
03-33		INX	B-SP	Double precision increment register pair
DA	nnnn	JC	nnnn	Conditional jump to address nnnn where carry flag set
FA	nnnn	JM	nnnn	Conditional jump to address nnnn where sign flag set

D2	nnnn	JNC	nnnn	Conditional jump to address nnnn where carry flag reset
C2	nnnn	JNZ	nnnn	Conditional jump to address nnnn where zero flag reset
F2	nnnn	JP	nnnn	Unconditional jump to address nnnn
EA	nnnn	JPE	nnnn	Conditional jump to address nnnn where parity flag set
E2	nnnn	JPO	nnnn	Conditional jump to address nnnn where parity flag reset
CA	nnnn	JZ	nnnn	Conditional jump to address nnnn where zero flag set
3A	nnnn	LDA	nnnn	Load register A from specified address
0A-1A		LDAX	B-D	Load register A from computed address
2A	nnnn	LHLD	nnnn	Load HL direct from specified location
01-31	nnnn	LXI	B,SP,nnnn	Load sepicified double register with nnnn
7F-75		MOV	A,A-M,L	Move data to leftmost element from rightmost element
3E-36	nn	MVI	A,nn-M	Loar register with nn

00	NOP		No operation is performed by the CPU
B7-B6	ORA	A-M	Logical "and" reg with A
F6 nn	ORI	nn	Perform logical OR with the accumulator & the byte nn
D3 nn	OUT	nn	Send data from register A to specified port
E9	PCHL		Fill program counter with data from HL
C1-F1	POP	B-PSW	Load register pair from stack, set SP
C5-F5	PUSH	B-PSW	Store register pair into stack, set SP
17	RAL		Rotate carry/A register to left
1F	RAR		Rotate carry/A register to right
D8	RC		Conditional return from a subroutine,carry flag set
C9	RET		Return from a subroutine
07	RLC		Rotate bits left, set carry as a side effect

F8	RM		Conditional return from subroutine, sign flag set
D0	RNC		Conditional return from subroutine,carry flag reset
C0	RNZ		Conditional return from subroutine,zero flag reset
F0	RP		Conditional return from subroutine,sign flag reset
E9	RPE		Conditional return from subroutine,parity flag set
E0	RPO		Conditional return from subroutine, parity flag reset
0F	RRC		Rotate bits right, reset carry as side effect
C7-FF	RST	0-7	These restart instructions generate one-byte subroutine calls,given in the Z-80 operand.
C8	RZ		Conditional return from subroutine, zero flag reset

9F-9E		SBB	A-M	Subtract specified register from A with carry,as defined above
DE	nn	SBI	nn	Subtract immediate byte, the carry flag from accumulator
22	nnnn	SHLD	nnnn	Store HL direct to location e16
F9		SPHL		Fill stack pointer with data from HL
32	nnnn	STA	nnnn	Store register A into memory at e16
37		STC		Set the carry flag to 1
02-12		STAX	B-D	Store register A to computed address
97-96		SUB	A-M	Subtract specified register from A without carry
EB		XCHG		Exchange DE pair with HL pair
AF-AE		XRA	A-M	Perform exclusive OR with accumulator,byte
EE	nn	XRI	nn	Perform logical exclusive OR with accumulator,the byte
E3		XTHL		Exchange byte at stack pointer, register L

FOG — THE CP/M EXPERT

You've read the book and now will have a good, solid working knowledge of your Commodore 128. As you become more experienced, you will find out how much you can do with CP/M (and how much it can do for *you*) on your Commodore. But working with computers is never plain sailing. If you find you need any more help or clarification, there's an organization with a specialist's knowledge of CP/M—**FOG**.

FOG is a users' group for people using or interested in computers. The bulk of its support is to the CP/M operating system. More than 16,000 people worldwide subscribe to the monthly publication **FOGHORN**, which regularly runs to 80 pages and is wholly devoted to CP/M. Reprints of all back issues are available for a varying charge (depending on the issue) and two "best of" volumes have been compiled. Each year will see the release of a new "best of" issue.

A membership in FOG is $24 per year, and gives you access to all FOG services. As well as receiving the FOGHORN each month, members can draw from an extensive FOG/CPM Disk Library containing more than 300 disks and thousands of public domain programs. Other services include an RCP/M network that has more than 40 RBBS-RCP/M systems in operation, most of which accept both 300 baud and 1200 baud. In addition, a network of FOG-affiliated local groups meet at more than 300 locations. Special interest groups organized to augment the local group meetings cover such areas as dBASE II, ham radio operators, and Personal Pearl.

Another valuable FOG service is its technical hotline—a phone service provided by FOG's computer experts who give advice and assistance to callers. The hotline operates Monday to Friday 10am to 5.30pm PST. The phone number is **(415) 755-2000**.

FOG was founded in October, 1981 by a small band of early buyers of the Osborne 1. The primary purpose was to organize a library of public domain software to run on the O-1. A newsletter (which developed into the FOGHORN) was quickly became the focal point for the group's activities.

Today, as MS-DOS systems become more prevalent in the business world, and as many members have diversified their interests to both CP/M and MS-DOS operating systems, FOG recently began supporting 16-/32-bit systems through a new publication, the **FOGLIGHT**, and another disk library.

FOG is headquartered in Daly City, near San Francisco. The postal address is:

FOG
Box 3474
Daly City CA 94015-0474

The office location is:

FOG
295 89th St.
Suite 304
Daly City CA 94015.

Index